YOUR
FINANCIAL
REVOLUTION

DANIELLE HOWARD, CFP®, QKA®

YOUR FINANCIAL REVOLUTION

TIME TO RECOGNIZE, REVITALIZE & RELEASE YOUR FINANCIAL POWER

Published by Advantage, Charleston, South Carolina.
Member of Advantage Media Group.

ADVANTAGE is a registered trademark, and the Advantage colophon is a trademark of Advantage Media Group, Inc.

Printed in the United States of America.

10 9 8 7 6 5 4 3 2 1

ISBN: 978-1-59932-826-3
LCCN: 2017946904

Cover art by Owen Mortensen.
Cover design by Katie Biondo.
Layout design by Megan Elger.

This publication is designed to provide accurate and authoritative information in regard to the subject matter covered. It is sold with the understanding that the publisher is not engaged in rendering legal, accounting, or other professional services. If legal advice or other expert assistance is required, the services of a competent professional person should be sought.

This book is designed for informational purposes only and should not be considered a recommendation or investment advice in any way. Any financial decisions you make should be made based on your current financial situation and in consultation with your tax and financial professionals. This book is not intended to be considered tax or legal advice and should be considered the opinions of the author solely at the time of publication.

 Advantage Media Group is proud to be a part of the Tree Neutral® program. Tree Neutral offsets the number of trees consumed in the production and printing of this book by taking proactive steps such as planting trees in direct proportion to the number of trees used to print books. To learn more about Tree Neutral, please visit **www.treeneutral.com.**

Advantage Media Group is a publisher of business, self-improvement, and professional development books. We help entrepreneurs, business leaders, and professionals share their Stories, Passion, and Knowledge to help others Learn & Grow. Do you have a manuscript or book idea that you would like us to consider for publishing? Please visit advantagefamily.com or call **1.866.775.1696.**

I would like to dedicate this book to the One who has given me the lifelong path, unfolding the passion and the proficiencies to share with my family, friends, clients, and readers.

TABLE OF CONTENTS

III – SUMMER: ACCUMULATION

IV – FALL: DISTRIBUTION

V – WINTER: LOSS AND LEGACY

ACKNOWLEDGMENTS

I am still on my financial journey and partaking day to day in the financial revolution that is unfolding. To my parents, Bill and Bea—I extend my heartfelt gratitude for the financial opportunities and challenges that you walked me through as I grew in maturity. Your openness about monetary matters and willingness to talk has inspired me. To my husband, Mark—you endured my "financial policeman" phase and went along with my giving beyond safe bounds. We have grown so much and are financially stronger because of it. To my daughters, Jessica and Tamarah—you have heard more than an earful about money over the years, and this book will not be the end to it. To Molly, my office goddess—thank you for cheerleading and keeping my life sane through this process. To dear friends who have walked alongside, listened, encouraged, and given insight and wisdom along the way. I am also humbled and honored for the multitudes of meetings with other financial professionals who have graciously shared their wit and wisdom. To the clients who have walked through our doors, thank you for allowing me into the intimate spaces of your financial life.

INTRODUCTION

One day a man was walking along the beach when he noticed a
boy picking something up and gently throwing it into the ocean.
Approaching the boy, he asked, "What are you doing?"
The youth replied, "Throwing starfish back into the ocean. The surf is
up and the tide is going out. If I don't throw them back, they'll die."
"Son," the man said, "don't you realize there are miles and miles of
beach and hundreds of starfish? You can't make a difference!"
After listening politely, the boy bent down, picked up
another starfish, and threw it back into the surf.
Then, smiling at the man, he said, "I made a difference for that one."

—LOREN EISELEY

As a Certified Financial Planner and financial advisor over the past twenty years, I've been fortunate to make a difference, one person or one family at a time. I meet with people, get to know them, educate them, encourage them, ask them some tough questions, pose new opportunities, hold them accountable, and slowly help them keep their personal financial lives moving in the right direction. While the starfish story inspires me, I feel compelled to reach more people sooner rather than later.

Now is the time. With technological advances and the increasing disconnect from our financial decisions, the obstacles are greater and the consequences more imminent and impactful, for better or for worse. We have moved from using cash to credit cards to pushing a button or swiping our phones and no longer "feel" the pain of parting with our hard-earned money.[1] We don't discern the difference between soul needs or ego wants. We have given our power away to the marketers and media and the elusive idea that happiness can only be attained through self-indulgences. Innocently or intentionally, everyone's financial decisions have consequences—a pebble dropped in a pond whose ripple is felt around the world. As it has been for centuries, money is wound intrinsically throughout every critical issue facing humanity. As a result, the lack of emotional, physical, spiritual, and relational health around money exterminates true productivity and healthy, sustainable economic growth.

For example, when the Government Accountability Office picked through the debris of the financial crisis of 2008, it concluded with some surprising estimates of the economic cost of the Great Recession, with speculation at the top end reaching $10 trillion and counting.[2] Accounting for total economic losses, from output to unemployment, economists at the Federal Reserve Bank of Dallas estimated that the two-year recession cost every American at least

---

1   Utpal Dholakia, "Does It Matter Whether You Pay with Cash or a Credit Card?" Psychology Today, accessed June 9, 2017, https://www.psychologytoday.com/blog/the-science-behind-behavior/201607/does-it-matter-whether-you-pay-cash-or-credit-card.

2   Eduardo Porter, "Recession's True Cost Is Still Being Tallied," *The New York* Times, accessed June 9, 2017, https://www.nytimes.com/2014/01/22/business/economy/the-cost-of-the-financial-crisis-is-still-being-tallied.html?_r=0.

$20,000.[3] Even more alarming was the realization that global markets had become so intertwined that an international domino effect ravaged most of the major economies the United States depended on for support in times of economic strife. The findings made the 2008 recession the biggest economic mess since the Great Depression, spit thirteen million workers into the unemployment line, and battered domestic commodity production for generations.[4]

No one was immune from this economic pandemic, and we do not want to forget the pain inflicted. Winston Churchill and others have cautioned: "Those who fail to learn from history are doomed to repeat it."

We need to learn and shift course. We need to revolt against the norms recognized in society and entrenched in our psyche. We need to ignite and fuel the idea of using our money differently. We need to work together, harnessing the vigor of the human spirit and each of our unique abilities to rise out of our accustomed status quo. Have we become uncomfortable enough? Have we experienced enough financial pain to think of something beyond ourselves and cultivate a new conversation around what money means to us and what it can do for us? Have we learned that more stuff doesn't equate with more happiness?

Healthy, vital relationships with money and the choices made will birth thriving families. The ripple effect will be felt in businesses, communities, and nations. I see it as my privilege and duty to help set the stage for a healthy perspective on money and the roles it plays

---

3   Tyler Atkinson, David Luttrell, and Harvey Rosenblum, "How Bad Was It? The Costs and Consequences of the 2007-09 Financial Crisis," Federal Reserve Bank of Dallas Staff Papers, July 2013, http://dallasfed.org/assets/documents/research/staff/staff1301.pdf.

4   Center on Budget and Policy Priorities, Chart Book: The Legacy of the Great Recession, last updated May 30, 2017, http://www.cbpp.org/research/economy/chart-book-the-legacy-of-the-great-recession.

in life. There are others speaking to this as well, and together, as we bring a collaborative conversation to people who are hungry to use their dollars differently, I believe we will see profound change.

In this book, we'll explore the four primary areas of your financial life: (1) how money comes to you; (2) how you decide to share and give it away; (3) what you do to nurture, protect, and grow it; and (4) how you spend it intentionally within safe boundaries.

Recognizing, revitalizing, and releasing the full power of money to accomplish what is most important allows you to live in financial integrity. By the end of our journey together, it is my hope that you will not only have a clear vision of what true prosperity means to you but also some ideas on the tools, techniques, and temperaments needed to attain it.

A NOTE ON FINANCIAL SEASONS

Born and raised in colorful Colorado, I love the distinct change of seasons. I have even come to embrace that we can experience all of them in one day—in fact, many years back, here in our small mountain town, we had snow on the fourth of July and seventy-degree weather on the fifth.

Just as there are weather seasons, we have economic and life seasons for which we need to prepare. Both economic and life seasons follow somewhat consistent patterns. They are each distinct, yet they can exist hand in hand or have elements that throw us off from what we anticipate. If we are to capitalize on them fully and get the most out of our lives, we need to acquire a deep understanding of, and appreciation for, each season's characteristics, opportunities, and challenges.

Terms we often use for economic "seasons" include *early expansion*, *late expansion*, *early contraction*, and *late contraction*. Alternatively, we may refer to *innovation*, *boom*, *maturing boom*, and *shakeout*, or, more relatable, to *birth*, *growth*, *decline*, and *decay*. But no matter how it is worded, we experience unmistakable periods in the economy in fairly predictable order.

We also experience "seasonal" changes in our personal lives. Like the seasons in nature, change in our life seasons is normal and needs to be embraced if we want to live life fully. In previous generations, for instance, when Social Security was first implemented and life expectancies were around seventy-four years, we had the "spring" of getting educated (either in school or through apprenticeships). We then had a "summer" that saw many people working in the same field or career for thirty or forty years. Beyond that, people spent a short time in the "fall" of their lives, where they might have harvested their savings and investments, then moved into their "winter" season, preparing for death and wealth transfers, and then passed away.

The times they are a-changin'! Demographic, societal, technological, and workplace trends have converged in recent decades. A different perspective on the seasons of life has emerged as a result, one that is much more fluid and flexible than what previous generations experienced.

No longer do people work in the same career at the same company for their entire working life, and no longer need they heed the artificially contrived norm to retire at sixty-five, either. With medical technology, advancements in health care, and other life improvements, we are seeing longer life spans, and as a result, life seasons are being rewritten. Career people taking sabbaticals, going back to school, or "rewiring" their career goals and personal purpose is now possible throughout life.

While life seasons are sequential (starting with birth and ending in death), we may now experience a financial fall (needing to harvest what we have saved) earlier in our lives. Likewise, we can experience a financial winter (loss of a job or loved one) during our summer growth and accumulation season. We need to build wealth in different areas, such as real estate, stocks, bonds, alternatives, and good old-fashioned savings. Understanding the proper types of insurances to shift the risk of financial hardship, living within our means, and staying away from consumer debt will also serve all of us well if there is an unexpected weather change in any life season! We need to prepare for what could or inevitably will happen, have reasonable expectations about what can transpire during these times, and embrace the essence that unfolds in each.

For the purposes of this book, we'll look at elements of each life and financial season—which I break down into **spring**, **summer**, **fall**, and **winter**—and what you can do to recognize, revitalize, and release your financial power in each.

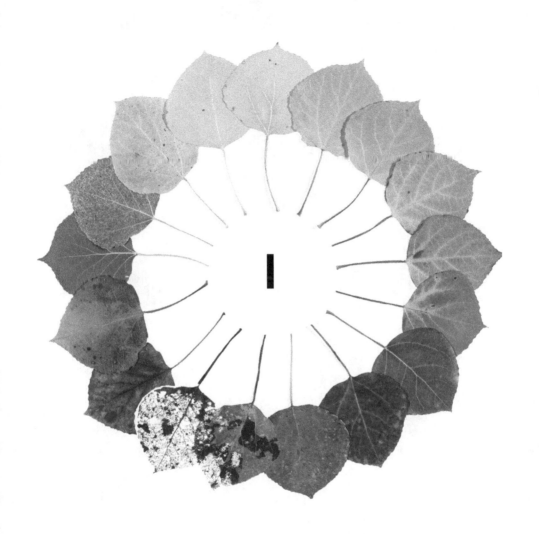

I

THE NATURE OF MONEY

CHAPTER 1

LET'S GET DOWN TO EARTH

Money is defined by its functions. Anything is money,
which is used as money: "money is what money does."

—SIR JOHN HICKS

Money means many things to each of us. It moves through our lives in various ways. It comes in fluctuating amounts through differing means, at various times, to support a multitude of purposes. In the philosophical sense, money is impossible to define. We all experience money differently. We can, however, strip the concept of money down to its most basic function for a simpler picture of its role in our lives. Its fundamental purpose is to serve as a **medium of exchange and a unit of value**. Instead of bartering for what we need or want, where people need to be exchanging at an exact time or place, we can use money as an intermediary. In that way, money is simply a unit of value that provides us with a standardized process for trade because its worth is universally accepted.

But, as we all know, money is much more complicated than its technical description. The ways in which money influences our physical, emotional, and spiritual well-being are seemingly endless. In a spiritual context, money can be seen as a "flow of our intentions," as Lynne Twist describes in her book *The Soul of Money*. It is a reflection of our principles and priorities, a tool to facilitate the choices and comforts for a life we most desire. It is not right or wrong, but more and more, its nature is being misconstrued, mismanaged, and misused. Before we can use our money wisely, we have to learn to see money not as a simple medium of exchange but as an expression of self and, again, a flow of our intentions.

WHAT STANDS IN THE WAY: THREE FINANCIAL HURDLES

There are three primary hurdles to overcome as we seek to use money differently: *discontent*, *discomfort*, and *distrust*. Most of us will be unhappy with our financial life at some point. Whether disenchanted with our vision of money's purpose in general, or with our ability to obtain it in the ways we had hoped for, or with the amount of joy we receive from it, financial **discontent** will pay all of us a visit in some form.

We also receive a slew of mixed messages about money throughout our lives. Misinformation and simple misunderstandings riddle discussions around money, making any dialogue about it tedious and tense at best. Take this line of the Holy Bible from 1 Timothy 6:10, for example: "The love of money is the root of all evil." In complete context, the quote is a reference to the dangers of greed. But it's commonly misinterpreted as another popular phrase: "Money is the root of all evil."

For most people, money's distinction as a taboo subject creates a great sense of **discomfort** when discussing financial topics. Money is tied so strongly to feelings of self-esteem and sense of purpose that talking about it makes people uneasy, even embarrassed. It's just easier to avoid the topic—and the financial uncertainties, misunderstandings, and mistakes proceed unrestrained and without correction as a result. The idea of exposing who we are financially and being transparent about what we feel, know, and do with regard to something so intimate is a challenge that few enter into. We often forego the expertise that would help clarify and understand our financial choices, choosing instead to make decisions based on our emotions, instincts, and money histories. Reorienting ourselves to be more open about money is one of the first steps on our financial journey. Depending on our individual upbringing, personality type, and experience with money, recalibrating that mind-set may be difficult, but it is not insurmountable.

The financial arena is replete with **distrust**. Emotions around money include fear and greed, and the financial industry is where we see those emotions played out in plain view. Whether regarding the big wigs on Wall Street or the local advisor on Main Street, there is the perception that the financial industry is just waiting for its next victim. It doesn't help matters that the industry is increasing in complexity. Taxation, tools, and techniques used to accomplish financial goals have evolved, and the language or jargon commonly used in the arena seems foreign to most people.

The image of financial advisors has been badly damaged over time, worsening the general lack of awareness of their purpose and heightening skepticism about their intentions and motivations. This distrust is not unfounded or unreasonable. The Madoffs of the industry have proven all too vividly that there are wolves out there in sheep's clothing, and financial "advisors" promising a magical pill that will solve their clients' ills instead of providing them with a customized process to transform their financial experience have misled unsuspecting people and greatly harmed the profession's respectability. The resulting distrust has added a new obstacle to overcome for both advisors and those in need of guidance.

JOURNEY TO FINANCIAL HEALTH

The detachment from money's meaning in our lives, combined with the challenge of having real financial conversations and the mess the financial services industry has given us, has put us in uncharted territory. By understanding the many facets of money, however, we can turn this around. We can reconnect with the significance and importance of money in our lives. We can communicate honestly and openly about money issues. We can each find the right team of advisors that will put our interests first and protect us from the snake oil brand of advisors out there.

Creating financial health is a journey, not a destination. The goal of a healthy financial life is not attaining an ultimate number; it's about understanding why you want that number in the first place and what you do with all the numbers along the way. Fortunately, financial health and well-being is not dictated by how much money you have to start, but if you embark on the journey, it is more likely that your net worth and your self-worth will flourish.

Simon Sinek has revolutionized corporate culture and leadership conversations with the encouragement to "start with the why."

In your personal financial life, I urge you to do the same. What is your "why"? Why do you want to have financial health? Why do you want to build your personal wealth? In generations past, we heard "I want my children to have a better life than I did." I encourage you to dig deep, have conversations about it with the people closest to you. The "why" for creating and maintaining my personal financial health is that I have children, and I want them to have a good relationship with and respect for money as one component of their full potential in all areas of their lives. What is yours?

LET'S DISCUSS THE SEASONS

The parallels between financial planning and nature offer plenty of playful and helpful metaphors to explore and understand. Depending on the season of your life, and the season of the economy, the way money comes to you, how you give it away, how you grow and protect it, and how you spend it will all change, unfolding opportunities and challenges along the way.

Like the seasons of nature, personal financial seasons are cyclical, forming a series of revolutions throughout your lifetime. Whether you're just starting your financial journey or you've been on it for decades, you can experience many economic seasons throughout your life. You may also experience several different financial and economic seasons during each of your progressive life seasons. Let's take a brief overview of some analogies.

For me, **spring** is a time to plant my vegetable and flower seeds, put them in the window, and anticipate transplanting them outdoors, where I can watch them flourish before the harvest of fall. New life and new beginnings are all around, which means it is the perfect time to prepare the soil for planting. Get clear on what you want to grow, either in your garden or in your financial life. Spring is also a great time for developing the mind-set, attitude, and knowledge for "planting the seeds" of a healthy financial life. Financial literacy and math skills will prepare you well during this season. Above all, spring is the time to get the right tools ready for use, making sure you know what they are for and how they are used before you need them.

Other financial implications of new beginnings often equate to a time of monetary expenditure and investment. A financial spring may mean that you have decided to "plant" a new business or maybe start furthering your education to enhance your career. If so, you will need to spend some time preparing your soil, so to speak. That may come in the form of determining how much start-up capital you will need for your business and where it will come from or what your financial aid options may be as a student.

Summer is the season of growth and accumulation. Once the soil has been prepped with the proper tools and techniques, summer is a time to nurture what you have planted to ensure an abundant yield. Likewise, your financial "summer" is a time to work hard, cultivate, and tend to what is important. Your financial summer will bring new resources into your life, ideally building enough net worth to allow for investments and a healthy fall "harvest" when you need it. Summer is also a time to stay vigilant and prepared in order to protect and nurture what is thriving. It is vital to know how much to use now and how much to set aside for seasons that lie ahead. While easy to do, it's dangerous to expect that summer will never end. Doing so can have devastating effects on your financial health when a summer season eventually dries out, particularly if you're moving into the later stages of your life and career.

Ah, summer! Let's relish it, share it, and experience it in all its glory, but keep in mind that this is one season in many.

Fall is my favorite time of year. I'm grateful to live in Colorado, where the colors, the smells, the crisp night air punctuated by a warm fire all combine for a beautiful experience. I also look forward to the opportunity to turn inward, to reflect on and put to use what I have learned over the spring and summer.

Fall is also a time to harvest, and your financial "fall" is no different. This season deals as much with recreating and reflection as it does with repositioning your assets. Your financial "harvest" will entail the distribution or unwinding of what you have accumulated in a financial summer. A financial fall season may also be the move toward "rewiring" habits, attitudes, and strategies. It may see a job change, a health challenge, a child headed for advanced education, a wedding, or a family move. These are times you will tap into what you have stored up, set aside, and diversified in different areas. A fall harvest may be a short-term distribution such as paying for a wedding or educational pursuits, or it may be a long-term life transition where sustainability of your financial resources is paramount.

If you have worked diligently and sought advice from a reputable financial planner to guide you when warranted, you will reap the reward of spring and summer. Do you have a clear picture of what resources are available to you? You need to understand how the equity in your home, investments, Social Security, employer pensions, business holdings, and life insurance cash values can shift from the "accumulation stage" to a "distribution phase."

Winter leaves most people asking, "Is it over yet?" It's a time of hunkering down and bundling up. The cold moves in, streams freeze over, and trees and gardens fall bare. Life and financial winters can include job losses, economic downturns, divorce, serious illness, and death—all the really tough stuff in life. No one can ever be perfectly prepared for the winters of his or her personal or financial lives.

They are hard, many times unforeseeable, and oftentimes carry large financial consequences. But that doesn't mean you don't have tools at your disposal to make the winter more bearable. Insurance, savings, benefits plans, Social Security, diversified investments, and estate-planning tools like wills and medical directives can all be leveraged to do the best you can until the spring returns.

Your financial journey will pass through each of these beautiful seasons. It may span a lifetime, or you may have many financial seasons in a short amount of time. Unlike the seasons of nature that run their course every year, the time frames for economic and personal seasons are much less predictable. Financial tools can be used differently during each season. They need to be revisited often to determine if they are beneficial or detrimental to your financial health as the seasons change. Seeking advice from a trained professional will help you delve into the tools you have and how they are working or not in whichever season you are experiencing.

All seasons—economic, emotional, spiritual, physical, and financial—should be considered gifts. You need to embrace the one you are in, enjoy it when possible, learn from its potential, and be expectant that a new one is around the corner. Let's consider six life principals as you move through the various types of life and financial seasons.

1. FEW THINGS ARE WITHIN OUR CONTROL.

From a seasonal snowstorm to a cataclysmic hurricane, preparation has the potential to see us through, but many times we still need to experience the storm. So it is with our financial lives as well. We can do our best to prepare for and prevent disasters. We can have savings accounts and rebalance our investment portfolios to adhere to our individual risk aversions, but we also need to be ready to ride out the waves of economic seasons and the uncertainties of life.

2. DIVINE TIMING.

There is a time for every season. We may get a taste of an early summer, but we can't rush it. We live in an instant gratification world, and we want everything immediately. It is a challenge to wait for the fruits of our labor, as seen in the proliferation of "get rich quick" schemes. We need to embrace the reason and unpack the glory of each season. We need to be careful not to rob others of the opportunity to learn from their seasons. George Kinder in his book *Seven Stages of Money Maturity* delves into the benefits of each magnificent stage. He shares that in financial infancy, we experience the pain of poor choices and learn to make different decisions moving forward. He walks his readers through to financial maturity, to "Aloha," where giving flows as freely as a summer stream.

3. GIVING IS FOUNDATIONAL.

We have all experienced the beauty of a sunset or flowers bursting forth in full bloom. Nature is a benevolent, abundant giver. We need to hold our lives open to receive and to let go. In our giving, many times we do so financially if there is something left over. By cultivating an abundant mind-set and understanding the flow of money, we can free ourselves to give and receive in a dynamic, honorable way. By embracing and nurturing a mind-set of contentment, we will produce the fertile soil of giving and enjoy the profound rewards. We can educate ourselves as to ways to leverage our giving with donor-advised funds, charitable remainder trusts, giving of appreciated assets, and other strategic tools. While rewards of tax minimization are nice, altruistic behavior also releases dopamine and endorphins that lead us to physical health and inherent happiness.

4. KEEP GROWING.

The seasons are perpetual. From sowing the seed, reaping the harvest, enjoying the cornucopia, and preparing to plant again, the virtuous cycle continues. Inherent in all of us is a quest to create, to become our best, and to continue to bloom. How do you grow perennial net worth and a generational mind-set? Diligence, hard work, and gleaning the wisdom of sage advisors will keep you flourishing.

5. WE NEED TO USE OUR RESOURCES WISELY.

We only have one earth. If we abuse it, it isn't sustainable. Nature is economical and efficient. A lion will eat what it catches, hyenas will finish it off, dung beetles will find usefulness in, well, you know—dung. With our financial resources, alignment with our core values will help us to create a sustainable economic ecosystem. We create suffering in our economies when we are wasteful, selfish, and hoard excess. We need to define "how much is enough" in every season of our financial lives.

6. THE INTERCONNECTEDNESS OF IT ALL.

We are all connected. Even miniscule species in nature play an integral part in the whole. It is the same with our financial lives. We have a responsibility to manage and make choices that consider the whole to keep the system working well. Your net worth does not define your self-worth. You are an important part of the whole, so you need to explore and find your element. If you put a horse in the middle of the ocean, it will eventually drown. The same is true when we are not living in integrity with our work or how money is coming into our lives. We need to look at our economic structures and move from the "ego economy," based on a scarcity mind-set and competition, to a true "eco-economy"—one that is based on cooperation and one in which collaboration values the well-being of all rather than just a few. We can do this in a free market economy, with healthy competition, to create better products and services and create new jobs. It may be challenging, but we need to create the environment where everyone has the opportunity to thrive financially.

CHAPTER 2

TIME TO TURN OVER A NEW LEAF?

*We cannot solve problems with the same kind
of thinking that created them.*

—ALBERT EINSTEIN

The economic crisis of 2007–2009 cut down the center of people's being, laying out the raw, vital organs of financial lives for everyone to see. Story after story filled our conversations and held us captive as we read the headlines. Like a doctor providing triage at the front line, financial advisors were trying to help people apply tourniquets and stop the bleeding or handholding clients by telling them, "Hang on; don't give in and sell now."

While those at the upper end of the wealth scale were affected, most of the damage was done in the middle to lower economic sectors. Main Street America had less robust financial buckets to dip into (savings, home equity, investments). They succumbed to fear as they sold investments at the worst possible time. Income disparity is increasing, and we now see how it was fed by the economic crisis. We saw benefits such as government bailouts going to the wealthy, while families in lower socioeconomic standing were sold toxic mortgages and experienced higher rates of bankruptcies and business failures.

In my years of experiencing many different economic cycles and guiding people on their financial journey, this was by far the scariest, most emotional, and most traumatic time. Everyone was affected. As a Certified Financial Planner practitioner, I witnessed heartbreak and I walked alongside people as they created new lives. Losing jobs, homes, relationships, and businesses was commonplace in my small community. Friends moved away to start anew. Households combined forces to minimize expenses. I facilitated conversations that tapped ideas and resources not considered when everything was going smoothly. This included taking loans from their 401(k) plans or partially surrendering cash value life insurance. We looked at how to manage new job training or restructure businesses to incorporate this economic season. Heaping plates of humility were passed around, and I took my share. I had never dealt with this type of chaos before. It was insidious and complex, and no one had all the answers. We had to get creative, moving forward slowly, not knowing what would unfold. People found and acknowledged strengths they didn't know they had. It was an opportunity to redefine the meaning of money in our lives.

VICTOR MENTALITY

In the powerful words of Viktor Frankl, "Between stimulus and response there is a space. In that space is our power to choose our response. In our response lies our growth and our freedom." It is not if but when something awful happens that we have a choice in how to handle it. Overcoming adversity is a chosen response to an unjust or unfortunate circumstance in our life—a response that only we can control. In other words, when faced with hardship or misfortune, we can either become a victim of it, or we can rise up and become a victor because of it.

One such example of a victor mentality is the story of Geneen Roth. Geneen, an author and behavioral counselor based in Nicasio, California, was one of the thousands of investors who lost their wealth to Bernie Madoff's infamous Ponzi scheme. She wrote about her experience in a book called *Lost and Found: Unexpected Revelations about Food and Money*. In it, she described how her insecurities around money echoed her unhealthy feelings about food.

She accepted her part in the painful incident, not that she could have seen what was going on but because she had abdicated her personal responsibility. "I do feel my part in this was my own lack of consciousness about money. Would I like to get that money back? Yes. But do I feel that what I've gotten since losing it has given me more wealth, in a way, than anything I had before? Yes." Was the financial crisis the bottom for many of us in terms of how we handle our finances? Was it painful enough to challenge the status quo over what true wealth is all about?

Was the financial crisis the bottom for many of us in terms of how we handle our finances? Was

**it painful enough to challenge the status quo
over what true wealth is all about?**

People have come through the agonizing haze of the economic
winter that started in December of 2007 and lasted until June of
2009. We will experience another brutal financial winter—it is not a
matter of if but when. Are there enough people who want to organi-
cally change the direction of their destinies? I think so, and if you are
reading this book, you do, too. Rather than capitulate and become a
victim, you are choosing to take the road less traveled. Congratula-
tions! You're embarking on the journey of financial health by building
a life based on your ideals and values and discerning what true wealth
means to you.

*You will find questions throughout the book to help you refine your
financial techniques, tools, and temperaments. Take the time to
reflect, answer, and discuss your thoughts with others!*

What is your "why"?

Why do you want to do your money differently?

What will your life look like if you start changing the trajectory
of your financial life?

What will happen if you don't change the direction of your dollar
decisions?

CLEAR SKIES WITH SOME TURBULENCE EXPECTED

No matter where each of us is at on our financial journeys, there are opportunities to explore and challenges to overcome. While we may have a destination in mind, it is the trek that will bring meaning to our lives. We can take steps to prepare. We can get comfortable enough to talk about, and create transparency in, our financial relationships. We can educate ourselves about what money is and when, why, and how we should use it. We may even get a good grasp of spending plans, asset allocation, diversification, and world markets. But even when we seemingly do everything right, it doesn't always work out the way we expect.

After the Great Recession, I had people tell me, "We thought we were doing the right thing. We were saving for the future, and now we feel further behind than ever." Money is emotional, and those waves of emotion can lead us to inflict worse pain on ourselves than warranted. Why do people capitulate to a down market and sell at the worst time? Why do people make financial decisions based on emotions or the talking heads on TV? We are human, and we need to have advocates in our lives to walk alongside us to help us think logically and analyze our options. Occasionally we are going to get some financial hurricanes or encounter some outliers that throw us all into an unknown environment. As in natural disasters, those who planned and prepared for financially cloudy weather definitely came out of the recession in better standing than those who did not.

Some people approach financial planning or creating a healthy financial life with distaste or disenchantment. "I don't want to know the inner workings of my money—that is the financial professional's job." Or, "Why save? The market will just take it back." Or, "I have more money than I will ever need. Why think about the future?" However, if we fully embrace that we are a vital part of the whole—that our daily decisions have a ripple effect that affects both those closest to us and those in the far reaches that we may never encounter—we may change our minds. We need to take responsibility for our actions. Day-to-day decisions have long-term impacts and implications.

WHAT IS MONEY GOOD FOR?

We need to define the meaning of money in our own lives. The fact that for so long we've been doing it wrong doesn't make the conversation any easier. The financial services industry has cooked up a tantalizing, yet unhealthy vision of our futures. For example, on retirement, what we have been fed is to garner as much money as we can and at age sixty-five sail off into the sunset, dressed in white linen, cocktail in hand. Research is showing, though, that a healthy transition to a fall life season is about becoming the next best version of ourselves and using our financial resources like the wind beneath our sails. It's about learning how to use money as a flow of our intentions and propelling our own individual life purpose and passions. Until you address your beliefs, attitudes, behaviors, and overall relationship with money and move it in a positive direction, you will find yourself stuck in the muck and mire of financial infirmity.

There is also an inherent overreliance on money for personal happiness in our lives. Money determines, in varying degrees, where we live, what we eat, how we look, how we feel, where we travel, whom we associate with, how safe we feel, and more. Money is interwoven into nearly every aspect of our lives. Because it's so important, it has a great impact on how society sees us and therefore how we see ourselves. It's virtually impossible for money not to affect our personal happiness, but how much it does and in what ways is completely up to us.

In 2010, research psychologists Daniel Kahneman and Angus Deaton of Princeton University found that money does buy happiness in the context of emotional well-being but only up to a point. You will eventually experience the "Law of Rising Expectations and the Law of Diminishing Returns." In his book, *What Your Money Means*, venture capitalist and philanthropist Frank Hanna shares the reality that the more money we have, the more we spend on goods or services. As we pay more for things or services, our expectations of satisfaction and pleasure rise and we become vulnerable to unhappiness, disappointment, and frustration when those expectations are not met. There is a point where our increased spending only increases the disparity between how much we have paid and what we get.

We need to use our money to survive and thrive, but more of it does not lead to more happiness. Take, for example, the country of Bhutan. It continues to rank first in the world in happiness equality when they measure their "gross national happiness," despite it not qualifying as a world economic power.[5] Research shows that the keys to happiness do not lie solely in having more money in the bank but in the powerful attitude of gratitude, mind-set of contentment, deep social networks, freedom to make life choices, and embracing generosity as a way of life.

You can start with creating a gratefulness journal. Every day, write down three things you are grateful for until it becomes natural for you to have an attitude of gratitude.

---

5 www.grossnationalhappiness.com

ℬ

Start writing down three things a day that you are grateful for.

BACK TO THE "WHY"

If the quest for more after a certain point will leave us feeling empty, what is it about?

Alden, in his early eighties, retired nearly twenty years ago from his engineering career and now spends a lot of time researching investments and trading in the market. His wife, Ann, in her late seventies, relishes her time teaching at a local health club, cooking for church events, and being available for family and friends. The couple is financially comfortable and content.

Alden says he enjoys making money in the market because it keeps his mind sharp, it's fun to do, and it's helped him to lead a full life, doing amazing things. Press him for a deeper answer, and Alden will say that Ann and the kids are givers—they are generous with their time and their financial resources—and it makes him feel good that he can manage their finances to keep that going.

For a long time, Ann didn't know her husband's true "why." She always figured he sat in front of his computer for his own fun—not to fuel what gives her the freedom to teach and help others. When they finally had this open, soul-bearing discussion, it changed her perception of him profoundly. These are powerful moments in our relationships.

How can you discover your true "why" and how it will change over the course of your financial journey? American psychologist Abraham Maslow and his "hierarchy of needs" theory may be able to help with that question. Maslow breaks down human needs and desires into a pyramid-shaped set of priorities, and it serves our purposes nicely as a quick-fire guide for identifying where you are and how you can find your "why" at various stages.

MASLOW'S HIERARCHY OF NEEDS

Physiological—sustenance, sex, sleep, and homeostasis

Safety—security of person, employment, resources, health, family, and property

Love and belonging—friendships, family, and intimacy

Esteem—achievement, respect of and by others, and confidence

Self-actualization—creativity, spontaneity, morality, and problem solving

HIERARCHY OF A FINANCIAL LIFE

Struggling. Basic life necessities are all you can afford. Prioritize needs versus wants and hone in on what is truly paramount in your financial decision making. Discipline and delayed gratification will serve you well here. Focus on eliminating high-interest and short-term debt. Your personal character assets of creativity, diligence, and resourcefulness will serve you well here.

Surviving. Necessities are met and debts minimized. Look at opportunities to create an emergency fund and live below your means in order to build financial momentum. You look at insurances and the opportunity to create various "safety nets."

Stable. Necessities are met, and you're free from consumer debt. You start to have some "wiggle" room and freedom in your spending choices. There is the opportunity to spend on "wants." This is the time you can start looking at making larger purchases such as an appropriately sized home. Start saving for future spending and ensure that risk management pieces are in place. New financial knowledge needs to be acquired as the complexity and opportunities of your situation grows.

Secure. You have the ability to diversify investments and really address "how much is enough" for your current use and refine what your needs are for future seasons in life. Giving can become a bigger part of your life as you find happiness in ways that are not associated with material gains.

Surplus. Investments are properly positioned and producing profits. You're living in abundance. Start dreaming, making sure you are using financial resources to live a life without regrets. You have the opportunity to give more, impact others, and focus on preparing the next generation.

As with Maslow's hierarchy, there are not delineations or demarcations of financial beliefs or behaviors at each level of peoples' financial lives. I have encountered people in survival mode who have a "surplus" mind-set and will share whatever they have with you. I have worked with people who financially should be at the "surplus" stage but who have not connected with a deeper "why," and the quest for more keeps coming up lacking. You must set to task with intention, diligence, and discipline to rise through this hierarchy. You may never have had to struggle, or survive financially, or moved quickly through the stages. I encourage you to reflect on this hierarchy. It creates empathy for others on their journey and an encouragement in the process of growth that allows you to bloom into your full potential. Just as a caterpillar must struggle through the process of metamorphosis, unassisted to become a beautiful butterfly, you, too, can become the next best version of yourself.

SHARPEN YOUR TOOLS

Regardless of which financial or life season you may be in, reevaluating your relationship with money is an ongoing task. Look honestly at the areas of life where money impacts you, and get to your "why."

- 🌰 What does it mean for you to bring money into your life with dignity, integrity, competency, grace, and joy?

- 🌰 How would it feel to give of your financial resources with guts and gratitude?

- 🌰 Why do you want to cultivate, grow, and protect your financial garden with diligence, wisdom, and care?

- 🌰 When do you want to create a plan that allows you to spend within safe boundaries and with joyful intention?

CHAPTER 3

CULTIVATING WISDOM

Knowledge is recognizing the street is one way.
Wisdom is looking both directions anyway.

—UNKNOWN

With the Internet at our fingertips, knowledge is easy. We can garner information from a seemingly endless list of resources at any time. In the general sense, knowledge and wisdom have rather broad definitions. Knowledge is composed of facts and truths gathered through investigative research, in-depth study, thorough dissection, patient observation, or life experience. Given the resources at our fingertips, we need to be discerning browsers, considering *where* we are obtaining our knowledge nearly as carefully as we consider the knowledge itself. The foundational beliefs and worldview on which we base our truths will decide what information we instinctively find appealing. But to understand a particular issue from multiple angles, we need to curate our knowledge more purposefully, selecting diverse, yet credible sources for our information stream.

Wisdom refers to the ability to dissect, discern, and disseminate that knowledge in a judicious manner, for the benefit of ourselves and for the betterment of the whole. Wisdom may be considered the practical, pragmatic application of knowledge in order to make good decisions in life. Wisdom is embracing the meaning of that knowledge, why it is important, and its impact on our own lives and the lives of others.

In the financial sense, **knowledge** is knowing what financial decisions make us happy. It's having the financial literacy to understand what tools we need to create a spending plan or to create different buckets to hold our future spending. There are a variety of apps to help us track our spending. We can all do the homework on the difference between a traditional IRA or Roth. We can get involved with employer-sponsored retirement plans and understand what choices we have for investment allocations and contributions.

Wisdom, on the other hand, is knowing that while certain financial decisions provide us with momentary pleasure or bliss, true happiness is not incumbent on externalities. Wisdom tells us that happiness is often a choice that only we can lay claim to—a feeling that is drawn out from deep within ourselves rather than from outside of ourselves. Financial wisdom comes from bringing money attitudes and habits into the light to determine what is working and what is not. Financial wisdom is recognizing that "when I pay myself first, I am creating future choices that will provide freedom." Financial wisdom is recognizing "my belief that more is better is holding me hostage to debt, and I have the power to change that belief and take action to eliminate the debt, providing me with peace of mind." Financial wisdom is knowing that "as I communicate with my family about our wealth transfer and estate planning intentions, I am creating possibilities for generational financial health."

What other examples of financial knowledge or financial wisdom can you think of?

We have been admonished to be judicious about knowledge and wisdom throughout history. Proverbs 13:20 tells us, "He who walks with the wise grows wise, but a companion to fools suffers harm." Or Proverbs 14:1: "The wise woman builds her house, but with her own hands, the foolish one tears hers down." Thomas Jefferson observed, "Honesty is the first chapter in the book of wisdom." And George Bernard Shaw warned, "Beware of false knowledge; it is more dangerous than ignorance."

You can dismiss it or tell yourself that you already know about money, but do you? Financial opportunities and challenges change exponentially by the day. While you do not need to know everything (nor can any of us), dive in and surround yourself with trustworthy advisors who will walk alongside you to educate, encourage, and guide you along the way.

You may want to increase your knowledge in measurable ways. It may be in areas related to the current economic environment: How do rising interest rates affect my portfolio? Are bonds as safe as I thought they were? What investments may perform better in the economic season we are headed into? How do taxes impact what investments I want to make? What will inflation do to my purchasing power? Financial knowledge and wisdom are the tools needed to be proactive instead of reactive in life.

Financial knowledge and wisdom are the tools needed to be proactive instead of reactive in life.

As wealth increases, increased knowledge is pragmatic and discerning wisdom is paramount. How do you prepare heirs for what will be theirs someday? If you love your children equally, how do you treat them uniquely? How do you structure your business or title assets to best accomplish the legacy that is important to you? How do you create a giving plan that reflects your intentions and leverages your giving? Are you up to the challenge to pursue and expand your knowledge base, then contemplate and convert it into wisdom to benefit your own personal growth and those you care about? These are difficult questions, but they will unfold insightful answers.

Your quest for wisdom may need to start by exploring your money mind-sets. What are your attitudes around money, and how do they affect your behaviors? What do you want your life to look like down the road? What will be the effect on others if you do, or don't, address opportunities or concerns? How can you have better communication about financial matters with those you care about?

Author and motivational speaker Wayne Dyer shares, "Our lives are the sum total of the choices we have made." As we all know, money profoundly affects every area of our lives—mental, physical, spiritual, and relational. Making it an ongoing practice to glean financial knowledge and wisdom will have a profound impact on every area of your life. Look at it this way: Without financial literacy, money is harder to get. Without financial planning, money is harder to keep. Without financial wisdom, money is impossible to truly enjoy, cultivate, and share with others.

SHARPEN YOUR TOOLS

Wisdom is found in the wake of knowledge.

- In what area of your financial life would you like to procure new knowledge?

- What steps will you take to move forward with your quest?

- Who will encourage you or hold you accountable for your learning objectives?

- Why is it important to glean wisdom around financial matters?

SPRING: PREPARATION

Spring is the season of new beginnings. The spring season of life includes births, graduations, weddings, and new careers. A financial spring can occur at any life stage and would include income from a new career or entrepreneurial activity. It may be a new home or investment purchase. In both life and financial seasons, spring is the time that births beliefs and attitudes—the time to cultivate knowledge, skills, and beliefs. It is a time to establish relationships and resources. It is the season to set tools and techniques in place to maximize the opportunities to realize your true wealth.

CHAPTER 4

READY TO BLOOM?

Bloom as if you want to make the whole world beautiful.

—DEBASISH MRIDHA

I love springtime. The dawning of spring in particular is one of my favorite times of the year, as the warm sun pushes winter away and new life surrounds us. It is the time for nature to start anew or reawaken from its winter slumber.

Spring is a time when nature lays the groundwork for new growth, maximizing the opportunity to survive and thrive in what the future seasons have in store. Think of your financial life in the same way. Spring is a time to prepare your financial soil and sow the seeds in order to enjoy and reap the rewards in future seasons.

BUILDING ON YOUR STRENGTHS

What area of your financial life would you like to improve? This may range from the technical aspects of investment savvy or financial literacy to the softer side of communication or relationships with others around monetary issues. You may want to start a new career or build a new business. Do you want to take charge of your financial life instead of being the victim of circumstance?

We all have areas that need improvement. Each of us is a work in progress. Remember the old saying: It's the journey, not the destination that brings fulfillment. Each day, we can make different choices about our beliefs, attitudes, and ensuing actions. Each day, we can choose to change our trajectory.

A great way to build momentum is to look at the areas of your life where you have been successful. Ask yourself what led you to develop in that competency. Are there skills or behaviors that you learned from your family or place of origin? What life lessons (positive and negative) have played a part in your growth? Did you set goals? What attitude did you embrace? What time commitment did you make? What disciplines did you put into place that moved you forward? How were you held accountable? What support and encouragement did you get along the way? You should be learning and growing from your mistakes or failures, but if you find inspiration in your successes, you can gain even more by learning from what you did right.

I often look at my physical life as paralleling my financial life. I know that if I want to have a healthy body, I need to be intentional about exercise and diet, constantly making changes to fit my situation during different seasons of my life. The same can be said for my financial life. There is no perfect recipe or illusive "ten steps to success." We have all heard "eat a balanced diet, low in saturated fat and processed foods, and get regular exercise" as a foundation to health. We have also heard "spend less than you earn, avoid consumer debt, maintain liquidity, set long-term goals, and save toward them" as foundational to our financial health. In both of these situations, we all need to dig deeper and look at how to build on those foundations for each unique situation.

Look at your life and celebrate what you have accomplished. You won't stop pursuing excellence in those areas; you will continue to build on them as you get constructive feedback. With a realistic view of your financial life, the areas you would like to improve upon will become clear. New opportunities will unfold in the areas you want to pursue. Apply the techniques, skills, knowledge, and attitude that have helped you in other areas of merit.

FREE TO SOAR: CREATING A POSITIVE MIND-SET

Don't let negativity hold you back! The news media is predominately doom and gloom, day in and day out, and personally we often tend to dwell on our inabilities and a mind-set of lack. Whether at the macro level (what is happening in the worldwide market) or at the micro level (personal circumstances, challenges), we may focus on the negatives, and our consciousness can be consumed with fear, anger, regret, and resentment. Unless we recognize and acknowledge when we are having these thoughts and make a conscious effort to change or redirect them, we will likely hone in on limitations and obstacles rather than all the possibilities and options at our disposal.

But we can change direction! We can focus on positive aspects of our life. The science of neuroplasticity is showing us that we can actually rewire neurons to create new pathways in our brains to think differently. By reflecting on the positive aspects of our lives and the value of what we already have, we will likely create more of the same.

According to Lynne Twist, in her book *The Soul of Money*, "What you appreciate appreciates." Encouragement also comes from leadership guru Robin Sharma: "What you focus on grows, what you think about expands, and what you dwell upon determines your destiny." Try it! Share what you appreciate about someone and watch what happens.

How can you nurture this positive cycle? Reflect on specific areas of your life—family, community, finances, or health—and again ask yourself what you value most in each area.

What are your current "riches" in each of these areas?

What are the current successes you are having?

Spend some time thinking about it, write it down, and share it with someone close to you.

This exercise will help you appreciate what you currently have and create a picture of what that happy and satisfying life will look like. You may want to create a vision board or collage of what your ideal life looks like. Keep it handy and refer to it often. You will find yourself making different financial choices to keep you in alignment with your values and your goals.

Sometimes our ability to appreciate things is just a matter of perspective. Putting things in perspective allows us to see that we truly have much to be grateful for. I share this with you not because I have it down pat, but by keeping it in front of me I know I have a choice. Every day, I get to choose my attitude about the day. I get to decide how I want to spend my time, my money, and my mental resources. Life doesn't get any better than that!

How is your gratitude journal looking?

SHARPEN YOUR TOOLS

To improve your opportunities for success, reflecting on your strengths is a great way to find direction and motivation in your goals. Consider the following questions as a guide for planning your future successes.

- 🌿 In what area of your financial life would you like to bloom?

- 🌿 What would it look like to make a 5 percent improvement in this area?

- 🌿 What attitudes or skills are transferrable from other areas of success to your financial life?

- 🌿 What accountability structures do you have in place to reach goals and dreams?

CHAPTER 5

BEHIND THE MONEY: WHAT PECUNIARY PERSONALITY HAVE YOU PLANTED?

Know yourself. Don't accept your dog's admiration as conclusive evidence that you are wonderful.

—ANN LANDERS

In their book *Leading from the Emerging Future: From Ego-System to Eco-System Economies*, authors Otto Scharmer and Katrin Kaufer reference the three great divides we are currently facing: the ecological divide, the socioeconomic divide, and the spiritual/cultural divide. Money and financial decisions weave through the fabric of all these issues. They are not separate and cannot be addressed in a void. So it makes sense that by understanding money, we actually understand much more about the world in which we live and the people who are in it with us. Identifying our financial personalities—that is, how we interact with money and the inherent opportunities and challenges—will help us know ourselves and others and be more thoughtful around the flow of money in our lives.

Knowing who we are around money is a vital and foundational component as we "prepare the soil" for growth. Our financial personalities influence things like what careers we will be drawn to; what, how, and where we decide to give; our willingness to save and invest; and the risks we are willing to take. Understanding our behaviors and attitudes around money will guide our spending plans toward our values, influence how we converse with others about financial issues, and direct day-to-day decisions that have long-lasting impacts.

Dr. Brad Klotz and others have worked diligently combining behavioral and cognitive psychology with the financial field and economics to help us understand why we are so often irrational about money. We see behaviors that work against us in the stock market and in the supermarket. Recognizing our tendencies, triggers, and temperaments will help us manage our emotions in the financial realm.

FOUR MONEY PERSONALITIES

Throughout history, philosophers, scientists, social scientists, and theologians have used nature to help us understand ourselves. Aristotle, Empedocles, and Hippocrates used nature in classical writings. In biblical teachings, we see references to learning from nature and the natural elements found in humanity. Current scientific thought is gleaning new insight and wisdom from the examination and analysis of the physical world. As a thought-provoking exercise, let's look to nature for a perspective on the variety of money personalities that exist. Can you identify with a component of nature—water, earth, air, or fire—as a way to understand the benefits and drawbacks of who you are around money?

FIRE

Opportunities: You enjoy adventure and the unexpected. You are a natural entrepreneur who dreams big. You will invest in yourself and your passions. You attract others with your passion and intensity. You are entertaining and like to be with people. Your friends will join you on a moment's notice. You enjoy picking up the check and having people recognize you for it. You are attentive to the needs of others and like to give unexpected and expensive gifts. In your giving, you like to have your name on a plaque or publicly acknowledged. You will lend money to a friend in need. You spend your money on things that help you project that image.

Challenges: You burn through money quickly and can get caught up in debt when buying things you don't need. You may put all your financial eggs in one basket—either your entrepreneurial activities or investment strategies. Picking up on a hot stock tip and going "all in" excites you. No such thing as delayed gratification here—you just go for it! You may get burnt out at work because you give it your all. You lack savings or reserves because you are so optimistic about your success. You tend to keep money secrets from significant others. You can feel alone and isolated because you won't share your money problems with others. You may feel guilty or ashamed because of spending, because of how much you have "lent" to others, or because your "all in" investments didn't work out.

AIR

Opportunities: You are a thinker. You are resourceful and studious. You want to analyze your investment ideas and think through financial decisions. You will actually read *Consumer Reports* and delve into ratings on products you are considering. You are rational and proactive around financial matters. You can see the "big picture" of what you want your money to do for you. In your financial life, you will find a way to creatively solve a problem— whether it is finding a job, getting out of debt, or working toward a goal. While you can multitask, you excel when you are focused on a project, goal, or problem.

You are not pressured by others' expectations of what you should do financially. You may be seen as dancing to the beat of a different drummer when it comes to your purchasing decisions. You are comfortable with the impractical if you have thought it through.

Challenges: Just as the wind can change direction, so can you. You can be seen as insensitive, inconsistent, selfish, or dishonest. When you lack the skills and information to feel financially confident, you won't make a decision, and you may also be prone to "analysis paralysis," a state where there will never be enough information to make a decision. In giving, you may be disappointed if the money is not used exactly as you intended. Because you are a "big picture" thinker, it is hard for you to focus on the details—and you don't like the minutia of putting together a spending plan. You may have challenges supporting yourself as the sole financial earner, as you tend to pick fields that don't pay as well as other career choices. You may have challenges in collaborating with people in your life who are affected by your financial choices. You can feel trapped or financially obligated to others.

EARTH

Opportunities: You are solid, stable, and reliable. You want security. You are more comfortable with money under the mattress and have an inherent distrust of the "system." You have the spending plan, achievable financial goals, and ample savings. You set your mind on a financial goal and work hard to achieve it. You shop wisely for bargains. You feel secure with material possessions. You tend to be more conservative with your investments, seeing slow and steady as a desirable attribute. You are loyal, whether to your bank or to advisory professionals. You see saving now as spending choices in the future. You find it important to care for what you have. Delayed gratification is a game for you. You are organized. You are reliable and very pragmatic. You will be proactive in your financial life.

Challenges: You can be stubborn and bullheaded. You may stick with a job, investment, or financial product even though it is no longer helping you reach your potential. You can be rigid with the spending plan—needing to stick to it no matter what, leading you to miss out on opportunities. You tend to be a hoarder as you seek security, meaning, and comfort from material possessions. You tend to save for tomorrow and miss out on today. You are frugal to a fault when you buy on price point only, not on quality. You can minimize risk too much, in the market and in your earning potential. Earth personalities are slow to change and may not rebalance their portfolios or change their asset allocation as warranted. Better to stay safe than take a chance, you underestimate what impact inflation will have on your long-term needs. You may even sacrifice participation in social events because of the cost, a choice that may lead to feelings of isolation and loneliness.

WATER

Opportunities: You live in the moment. You are lighthearted, creative, and giving. Money flows easily in and out of your life, not necessarily in quantity but in context. When it is flowing in as a trickle, you will be ineffectual, but when the financial waters rise, you will be a force to be reckoned with. It is not something you pay too much attention to. You adapt easily to circumstances beyond your control. You hold on to things lightly, whether a job or your pocketbook. You can forgive others when they have financially wronged you. You share what you have easily with others. You are optimistic that things will work out fine and are great at going with the flow. You make financial decisions quickly, based on your feelings. You connect with people and can be very trusting. Financial details are not your strong suite. Others depend on you because you nourish their spirits. You look for what needs to be done and do it.

Challenges: You go with your gut, making emotional financial decisions, and that can work against you. You get excited about upward market momentum and buy in late, then get anxious when market corrections happen and get out at the bottom. Because you are trusting, you can also be gullible, falling for "get rich quick" schemes. You may give to a fault, sacrificing your own needs and security for others. Because you can feel pulled in many directions, you don't have a clear picture of what money means to you. You can be pulled by the need to "keep up with the Joneses" as you wrestle with your sense of identity.

We all have these four elements radiating and at work within us. However, based on our DNA, upbringing, and societal and environmental components, we may lean on or resonate with one elemental personality over another. None of these personalities is right or wrong, better or worse. They're just different, and they impact our financial lives uniquely as a result. We need to recognize who we are and the elemental personalities of the people in our lives who are affected by our financial decisions. The idea is to recognize, acknowledge, and build on the opportunities and temper the challenges of our personality to work toward balance for ourselves and those who are important to us.

OUR PERSONALITIES AND THEIR IMPACT ON OUR FINANCIAL LIVES

Our belief system comprises our spiritual, moral, social, intellectual, economic, and political beliefs and views. At a basic level, our beliefs are a collection of memories—influenced most of all by our DNA makeup, upbringing, and cultural influences—that shape our general attitudes about, well, everything. Starting at birth, we take in everything we see, hear, smell, feel, and taste and begin to make sense of the world around us. As we experience the world, we have an ever-growing collection of information to guide our decisions. From the financial context, it is important to look at our beliefs about money and whether they are serving us or hindering us with regard to reaching our full potential. I'll give you an example.

Aiden and Janet wanted to start growing their family. They could barely make ends meet and spent a lot of time arguing about it. They wanted children, but that seemed like a burden that could quickly wind up putting more stress on their marriage.

They wanted to know why they were arguing about money so much and couldn't stick to a spending plan or set goals. They needed a deeper historical perspective to find their answer. Janet came from a family where they didn't talk about money but always had enough to do what they wanted to do. If Janet asked for something, she got it. She never really knew where it came from, but because it was never an issue, it didn't seem to matter. Subsequently, she grew up thinking she never really had to worry about it.

Aiden and his sisters, on the other hand, were raised by his mother. He mowed lawns as a kid to earn his own money. One day, he caught his mom taking money out of his jar. It left him feeling betrayed and instilled an urge to spend his money before someone else did.

When Janet and Aiden looked back at those childhood memories and thought about how they were impacting their current situation, they each had a profound epiphany.

"I need to be aware of what we have and be responsible to use it wisely," Janet said.

"I spend my paycheck on things I think are important," Aiden said, "which may not be in alignment with what Janet and I should be doing together."

Looking at our past is a great way to rewrite our money scripts and discover a more effective way forward. We all become "creatures" of habit based on our belief systems, whether they are true or not. Once we believe something to be true, we will operate religiously unless we question the belief to determine whether it is serving us or holding us back from our potential.

Our beliefs form our values. Everyone in the world has "values." They are abstract principles that serve to guide the conduct in our lives, and they're very subjective. One person may value tradition, while another may value innovation. In the previous example, the reason why Aiden and Janet were having a money conflict is that their beliefs were not lining up with their principles. As the two discussed their values, they both focused on integrity and honesty.

I asked if they felt their behavior around money aligned with what they both valued. They both answered no. If our financial decisions are not a reflection of what we hold dear, then we need to change our belief systems before changing our behavior. Otherwise, the change will not be sustainable.

If our money "scripts" do not align with who we "essentially" are, or if our behaviors around money do not align with our personal values, there is a disconnect and we are at unease. As we discussed briefly in chapter 3, our financial decisions can actually have an impact on our physical, emotional, and spiritual health.[6] Ultimately, it's our values that inform our attitudes, and it's those attitudes that determine our behavior. These attitudes can be divided into three distinct components:

Affective. A person's feelings or emotions about a particular subject or object. For example, "Poor people are lazy," "Money is fun," or "Investing is scary."

Behavioral (natural tendencies). The way our attitudes influence our behavior. For example, "I don't give money to the homeless," "I buy what I want," or "I don't put money in the stock market."

Cognitive. A person's belief or knowledge about a particular subject or object. For example, "I believe poor people don't care," "Debt is just a part of life," or "You can't make money in stocks."

Those attitudes inform the actions we take in life. Sometimes they serve us well, and other times they hinder us from getting ahead. And while actions will become habits over time, they can be changed.

The concept of financial personalities is partly why talking about money is so difficult for many of us. Deep down, we know that how

---

6   Eileen Y. Chou, Bidhan L. Parmar, and Adam D. Galinsky, "Economic Insecurity Increases Physical Pain," *Psychological Science* 27, no. 4 (2016).

we think about and use money reveals our true selves. There's transparency and vulnerability inherently embedded in the conversation around money. We have friends who tell us how they're using their money to fund nonprofits or invest in companies that are benefiting the world. Other friends focus on themselves, touting the latest, greatest gadget or sporting the most recent fashions. Still other friends talk about financial stress—the high cost of living or the unpaid bills. Conversations about money expose our true values, our identity, and the realities of our life. What may seem like an innocent, casual chat can suddenly become a very intimate conversation and reveal more about ourselves than we want.

RECONNECTING YOUR MONEY AND YOUR VALUES

Check out your checkbook or your credit card statement and you'll see what you value. Look at where your money flows, and you will get a pretty good idea of what your life is about. You need to first look at yourself—for your own edification and for your own personal growth. Spend the time to keep track of your expenditures for a month or two. Then sit down and determine if they align with what is important to you. People don't like the idea of creating a "budget." It sounds limiting and comes from a scarcity mind-set. "We can't go out to eat; it's not in the budget." Instead, look at creating a **spending plan**. "We have $_____ to spend on eating out this month; where should we go?" In other words, tell your money where to go instead of asking where it went.

Upon reconnecting with your current choices, be prepared to wrestle with some of the things that come up. You may say to yourself, "Wow, I value security, but I am not putting any money away for emergencies or for my future spending needs." Start questioning yourself and be willing to take baby steps in a different direction.

You will need a clear picture of your financial personality—what money really means to you—before you will truly be able to talk about goals or start moving in the right financial direction.

Randy and Melanie are a perfect example. They had a pile of goals: sending their two kids to college, taking an annual vacation, and retiring in their early sixties were at the top of a long list. Simply crunching the numbers would be a waste of time without digging a little deeper into their personalities, mind-sets, and behaviors in order to create a practical plan that was plausible to accomplish.

Aside from having too many goals, the couple were terrible savers and were thousands of dollars in debt. Looking at the effect of their financial personalities, beliefs, and mind-sets about money as they had grown up, got married, and were maturing helped them realize that their financial behaviors were not reflective of what was truly important to them. They needed to rewrite their money script.

With that realization, they could start the slow process forward to address their debt, contribute to their children's educations, and create a spending plan that would work today and provide some savings for their future.

Meaningful, attainable goals were the only way they could move toward, but they also had to understand "why" it was important to create a healthy financial life. They wanted their kids to learn a different way of managing money and not experience the stress and tension they had. It was a lot of hard work and took over a year to really change their direction, but the education and empowerment they learned through the process has stayed with them.

Mike and Kathy had a different set of challenges. They had a pile of money and little clarity about the upcoming transition into the "fall" of their lives. They were uncertain about whether they had enough, and they still had kids to put through college. They had no idea how to use the variety of financial tools they had wisely to support them in what was truly important to them. Simply crunching the numbers would not address their "scarcity" mind-set. They needed to dig deeper. Mike had a business and had worked all his life, and while he enjoyed aspects of it, he was tired. Kathy was the beneficiary of a trust from her family and had never thought too much about money. Her belief system was wrapped around the message she received as a child: "Don't worry, this is too complicated for you."

Because the couple had always had the "safety net" of the trust, they never had to "mature" with regard to what it meant to have a healthy financial life. Now they wanted to do it differently—they wanted to "rewire." Living a life of leisure was not going to be fulfilling enough. What would bring purpose and intention to this next season of their life? Even though they had a big financial pond to swim in, they wanted to reconnect with what was important to them about money and use it wisely so that it would be sustainable for future generations. They wanted to use the variety of financial vehicles they had (insurances, retirement plans, equity in homes and businesses) more efficiently and effectively. They felt their kids were "entitled" and didn't want to send them out into the world ill equipped. They wanted to prepare their heirs for what would eventually be theirs to use wisely.

The journey of financial health can begin at any age. It's never too late or too early to learn more about your spending habits, attitudes, and behaviors. Chances are you will need to change something about them, but don't let that discourage you from discovering your true financial self. It's the only way you can take control of your life and start making the choices that align with your ideals.

SHARPEN YOUR TOOLS

Understanding your beliefs, attitudes, and inherent personality is the first step toward taking control of your financial experience. Take a moment to reflect on how your relationship with money began.

- 🌿 What money personality did you most relate to?

- 🌿 What is an early memory around money in your life?

- 🌿 What monetary message did that memory create?

- 🌿 Is that message serving you or hindering you in moving forward with financial health?

- 🌿 What message would you like to build upon?

- 🌿 What message would you like to rewrite?

CHAPTER 6

BEWARE OF THE WEEDS!

Unforgiveness is like drinking poison yourself and waiting for the other person to die.

—MARIANNE WILLIAMSON

During the spring, it is essential that I stay on top of weed control. In my garden, if I am not aware of the difference between a flower and a weed and diligent about keeping unwanted plants out of my garden, they can rapidly take over, choking out the life of what I want to bloom. In our financial lives, two of the most noxious weeds are entitlement and unforgiveness.

ENTITLEMENT

Entitlement grows in the soil of both plentitude and lack. With monetary dearth, an entitlement attitude can wreak havoc in a number of ways. We grow dependent on others, and over time, that dependency robs us of our self-esteem. As an advisor, I have heard stories of parents paying off their adult child's credit card bills or keeping them on the financial teat longer than is healthy. Doing so can keep children from embracing life's challenging seasons, defaulting to passivity and laziness. It can kill the drive to persevere or embrace a teachable moment. It squashes ingenuity and responsibility. It creates victims instead of victors, and the confusion of net worth for self-worth will ultimately carry demoralizing consequences.

At the other extreme, copious wealth can create an entitled, demanding nature in interactions with others, snuffing out the light that people share. A profusion of wealth can create the illusion that the rules don't or shouldn't apply or that rules intended for everyone's comfort can be disregarded because of financial stature. Expectations of others are unreasonably high, and there is no room for failure. It, too, confuses net worth and self-worth through self-aggrandizement; both extremes create equally sorrowful and painful outcomes.

Young or old, rich or poor, we can easily be swayed toward the mind-set of entitlement, where privileges are mistaken as rights and are then presumed to be the status quo. When we expect something for nothing, or think that someone owes us something because of our financial standing, the weed's roots grow stronger. It is a one-sided attitude based on taking a view completely out of balance with life's order of giving and receiving.

The entitlement mind-set starts as a small weed, but if untended, it will grow like cheatgrass, consuming the beauty of relationships and wreaking havoc on lives. It is a tenacious barrier to a healthy financial future, no matter where you lie on the spectrum of financial wherewithal.

We cannot let an entitlement mentality devour our financial gardens. We see it embodied in the Madoffs and Martin Shkrelis of the world, and sadly it lies in each of us. We must conscientiously and persistently use the right tools to keep it at bay.

The simplest, yet most profound tool to dig up the weeds of entitlement is gratitude, a virtue tool that needs to be used daily. When we look at our abilities, possessions, resources, relationships, and experiences as gifts that come from someone outside of ourselves, our view shifts dramatically. It helps us imbue humility, a sure determent to entitlement.

🌿

How is your gratitude journal looking?

Another way to combat entitlement is to keep the tools of compassion and empathy sharp. Actively engage in a perspective practice, such as reminding yourself to "walk a mile in their shoes." Take time to look at life from a different point of view, especially from the person who is most affected by your decisions. I see Scrooge visiting the home of Bob Cratchit with the Ghost of Christmas Present as a perfect example.

Maybe we can see it another way, too. Consider this: The world take-home daily pay is $1.82. That means that the average American's paycheck is in the top 1 percent of the world. Can that awareness change our perspectives? Compassion and empathy are strong weed barriers, protecting the growth of what we want in our gardens.

We all feel entitled at times, but if we can catch our thought process, it gives us pause and potential for change. Our culture of materialism doesn't help with that. We live in a world with the Internet and our phones and everything flashing in front of our faces telling us, "You don't have enough. You aren't enough. Keep buying. Keep consuming."

We're seen as consumers these days rather than citizens, as dollar signs instead of individuals. As a result, there's a growing disconnect. The consumer culture can deepen the disparity between the haves and the have-nots, leading us into the entitlement mentality no matter which end of the spectrum we find ourselves. Whether the entitlement of the wealthy or the entitlement of the poor, neither is right or beneficial to society.

UNFORGIVENESS

Another impediment to a healthy financial life that needs diligent tending is the noxious and poisonous weed of financial unforgiveness. This weed bloomed in my own life, and I had to dig deep to pull up its tenacious roots.

The biological father of my oldest daughter was killed in a motorcycle accident when she was seven. He had momentarily been in her life, and she had no memory of him, yet the emotional impact was multifaceted and deeply felt by our family. Then there was the financial impact. When I received a letter from the attorney representing his estate, I innocently thought they had my daughter's interest in mind. Since he had never paid child support and had an outstanding judgment against him, I expected to receive a check for all that was due my daughter. I was deeply mistaken. I did not seek legal counsel, and when I found out his estate had been settled and she would receive nothing, I was livid. I was furious with the "system" but mostly irate at myself for being so naïve.

Many hurts in life revolve around the expectations of ourselves and others to do the "right thing" as we understand it. Money hurts are no different. We feel justified in our broken relationships, bitterness, or resentments. The truth is, we are only hurting ourselves.

I had to do some soul searching and wrestle with what it meant to forgive financially. I was befittingly angry with him, the system, and myself. This was an infringement on a small child entrusted to my care. It was a violation of her financial rights. This was her college money, a future down payment on a home, something tangible from the man who was unable to be a part of her life. I slowly embraced that I had a choice. Part of me wanted to hang on to the anger—even when it was at myself. I could let this weed consume me, become resentful and bitter, or I could set myself free by forgiving and moving on.

Part of the process for me was to embrace gratitude in other areas of my life. I was resilient and resourceful. I had the support of my husband, family, and friends. I had faith that my daughter would have what she needed in life and a conviction that this "mistake" was not going to define us. I had to accept that I made an error and that others make them, too. We are human; we are fallible. I did the best I could with the knowledge I had, and I was determined to learn more and do better for myself and others. Forgiving didn't mean I forgot. The pain I experienced played a part in my desire to help others avoid financial mistakes and to seek assistance and expertise when I needed it in the future.

This was just one of many incidents in my lifetime where I have been hurt or I have innocently hurt someone else with my financial decisions. I know I am not alone. Know that *you* are not alone. The weeds of financial regret, resentment, anger, and unforgiveness have many seeds, and each can become firmly entrenched in your life.

Spiritual belief systems look at forgiveness as a vital component with the foundational belief that you are forgiven and capable of forgiving. If you are a person of faith, explore what needs to happen in your heart and your head in order for you to move forward with regard to financial forgiveness. There may be a ritual of confession, atonement, or appeasement that will guide you through the process.

We can also scan the horizon and be more introspective. In order to enjoy a healthy financial life, we need to absolve financial intrusions and move forward. Financial forgiveness can regard misdeeds by our government, Wall Street, and the Madoffs of the world, employers and employees, family and friends, and even ourselves.

"Forgiveness is a virtue of the brave," said Indira Gandhi. I couldn't agree more. We need to bravely face what it means to financially forgive and take the first step forward in doing so. I also appreciate the words of Paul Boese, "Forgiveness does not change the past, but it does enlarge the future." There's no question that money is an integral part of our lives. Forgiving ourselves and others will only help it to bloom, for us to enjoy and share with others.

SHARPEN YOUR TOOLS

As any gardener or farmer will tell you, keeping your beds and fields free of weeds, pests, and diseases is a full-time, year-round chore. But without it, nothing you want to grow and see flourish can or will. Being honest about your past financial mistakes or transgressions against you is the only way to root them out for good. The following questions will get you started in the right direction. Keep in mind that your mistakes refine you, not define you.

🍃   Do you have unfinished financial business?

🍂 What financial transgression have you experienced?

🍂 Have you innocently or intentionally used money as a tool to hurt others?

🍂 Is there a way you can seek forgiveness or extend forgiveness that will free you to move forward?

SUMMER: ACCUMULATION

Ushering in a time where life blossoms and grows, summer is the season of accumulation. Your life summer may find your family growing and your career thriving. Your financial summer will have your net worth increasing. Following a successful spring preparation, summer can be challenging, but if managed and cultivated well, it can bloom into the most rewarding season on your life journey.

CHAPTER 7

GROWING SEASON

*Each moment is perfect and heaven-sent, in that
each moment holds the seeds for growth.*

—SUZAN-LORI PARKS

The onset of summer signals the start of boating season for our family. We have been on the river in various incarnations of plastic tubing since my childhood. Many years ago we purchased inflatable kayaks and have been creating fun new memories on the water ever since. Wouldn't it be nice if our financial journey were as simple as putting the boat in the water and going with the flow? I wish it were that easy.

A summer river trip and life's financial journey have a lot in common. A successful experience with both entails planning and preparation. You must understand what you want to accomplish, and you must procure the tools with which you will achieve it. You may have a goal or destination in mind, and your perceptions of what your journey will look like may be admirable, but then you put your boat in the water and life happens. Time and again, life reminds us that goals require patience and determination. Goals provide guidance, but how we handle what actually happens on the journey will ultimately define a "successful" experience.

PLANNING AND FLEXIBILITY

One of my goals when we first started boating was to keep my kayak upright, with my body and gear always safely planted inside. After a particularly grueling spring runoff adventure, with fast water and major rapids, a dear friend with years of experience shared that getting "dumped" is part of the adventure. I had to plan on it and be prepared for what I needed to do to recover. I actually practiced flipping my boat so that when it did happen I would be prepared.

Reading the river is not easy, and neither is reading life. We pick our run and get into our boats with a "take-out" destination down-stream. We anticipate a pleasant journey, then hit an unexpected rock, flip, and lose our paddle. Likewise, we start our day, look down the road with enthusiastic anticipation at what we have planned, and wait for the payoff. Sometimes our plans don't go the way we'd hoped. Whether we get slammed with economic uncertainty, health problems, family dynamics, or some other unforeseen challenge, our lives and finances can turn on a dime.

Buried in the chaos is both distraction and opportunity. Which path you choose will be determined by your personal flexibility and attitude. We can succumb to the events that thwart our plans, or we can shift our perspective, look at what needs to be done differently, and keep moving forward. We need to trust the process even more than the plan.

When I talk to people about what **financial life planning** is, I start with what it is not. It is not a MapQuest formula, incorporating a starting point and a final destination to spit out the quickest route. The value in true financial life planning is looking at where you are now, understanding that where you are going is always moving and changing. Like shooting a rocket ship off to a distant destination, it is a matter of continuous course corrections to keep you on a trajectory headed toward an ever-changing future. Guiding those course corrections are your dreams, values, and fears, as well as the financial tools and resources available to you each step of the way.

> Like shooting a rocket ship off to a distant destination, it is a matter of continuous course corrections to keep you on a trajectory headed toward an ever-changing future.

To truly thrive in your summer season, flexibility is just as important as preparation. Just as you want the right gear for a river expedition, you want to have the proper financial tools for your life journey. You need to know how they work for you when things are going smoothly. When life happens and changes course, however, you also need to know how those tools can be refined, reworked, or replaced to meet those changes. Adaptability has as much to do with our attitudes as it does with our financial tools. When things don't go as expected, our emotional responses will set the course toward empowerment or defeat.

LEARNING HOW TO GROW WEALTH

Your financial summer is a prime accumulation season. It occurs after you have attained your foundational education and are moving into a career or to a new position within your career, or even when you are engaging in new investment opportunities. Maybe you're starting to build a family and defining what is important to you in that aspect of your life, or maybe there has been a shift in your family life. You may experience several financial summers in your life, like when children have left home or after the winter of a divorce or death of a spouse.

Growth for the sake of growth is the ideology of the cancer cell.

—EDWARD ABBEY

Accumulation is not solely focused on materialistic gain. The accumulation season is about deciding how to prioritize your financial decisions, paying yourself first so that you have spending for the future. It's a period focused on investments, the proper insurance for risk management, maintaining a steady income, and directing your cash flow to nourish what you truly value. Learning how to properly grow wealth and nurture your financial life with diligence, wisdom, and care is paramount in the summer season.

You want to be strategic and intentional about how to direct the money that comes into your life. Just as you look at a healthy physical life consisting of eating from the "pie" of proper proportions of vegetables, proteins, complex carbohydrates, and healthy fats, you can apply a similar strategy to your finances. With your disposable income, create an intentional spending plan to tell your money where to go. The monetary mindfulness "pie" consists of 10 percent toward charitable objectives, 10 percent into emergency and opportunity savings, 10 percent into longer-term investment strategies, and the remaining 70 percent for intentional living expenses. Notice the order. When you give of your financial resources first, it helps to keep your proper perspective on money in place. Your attitude will revolve around gratefulness and contentment, which will keep you from falling into the abyss of consumer spending. Next, pay yourself! This may initially include getting consumer debt paid off. You incurred these expenses, now take responsibility for paying for them. Both short-term and long-term savings strategies are vital for creating margin for the unexpected as well as opening options for your future financial freedom. Finally, look at spending the remainder in alignment with your values and what is important in your life. While this "pie" is a great place to start, you don't want to stop here.

As you thrive and grow in the summer season of your financial life, contemplate your decisions about how much is enough. What is the right size home? What is an appropriate vehicle? What kind of toys bring you pleasure, and how many? What are your spending lines in the sand? It is human nature that as our incomes increase, so does our standard of living. Up to a certain point, this is safe. However, we can capitulate to the materialism monster. Unwittingly, the more money we make, the more we are likely to spend on things that don't bring meaning to our lives or cause us to lose track of our intentions. Contemplate two important questions when making spending decisions: "Just because I can, should I?" and "Just because I don't have to, why wouldn't I?"

In economic terms, summer is usually the longest season, as we start enjoying the warmth of the season and get comfortable. We have good jobs, and so we start spending more than may be warranted by our needs and reasonable wants. We can start justifying our lifestyle with "I work hard; I deserve this." When we do, revisit the prior questions. It is a season to fully enjoy, but we can't forget to prepare for the fall and winter that lies down the road.

Always keep in mind that each financial choice you make will have implications later. This is known as the "opportunity cost." If you purchase a $5.00 coffee five days a week, you spend $100.00 a month, $1,200 a year. If that same money were put into an investment earning 5 percent compounding annually, at the end of twenty years you would have $39,642. Do you want that coffee (sweater, dinner out, set of golf clubs) today or do you want it tomorrow? Einstein called compounding interest the greatest creation of all time. It works well for you as you set money aside and works against you as you get entangled in consumer debt. Living in line with the 10/10/10/70 monetary mindfulness pie will help you to prioritize your financial decisions.

Strengthening your awareness that everything we do is interconnected is also important in the accumulation phase. Whether regarding the environment, our families and friends, our health, our local and global communities, or our financial future, our choices will impact much more than just our bank account balance. According to a report from the Natural Resources Defense Council, a family of four throws away between $1,300 and $2,300 worth of food per year.[7] A McKinsey study reported that household food waste is responsible for eight times the energy used in just producing the harvest.[8] This is because of the resources used to process it, bring it

7   "NRDC and Ad Council Launch New 'Save the Food' National Public Service Campaign," NRDC, April 20, 2016, https://www.nrdc.org/media/2016/160420.

8   Nicolas Denis, David Fiocco, and Jeremy Oppenheim, "From liability to opportunity: How to build food security and nourish growth," McKinsey & Company, accessed June 9, 2017, http://www.mckinsey.com/industries/chemicals/our-insights/from-liability-to-opportunity-how-to-build-food-security-and-nourish-growth.

to market, and prepare it, whether at home or in a restaurant. So not only is waste bad for your bank account, but it is also detrimental to our environment.

Each of us has an opportunity and obligation to make small choices that carry large impacts. Columbia professor and sociologist Robert K. Merton coined the terminology of the "law of unintended consequences," regarding outcomes of a purposeful action that play out in unforeseen or unintended ways. For example, buying groceries to put food on your table may be a seemingly innocuous action. An unintended consequence of throwing some of that food away is the amount of water that has been wasted in its production or other energy used for shipment.[9] From food purchases to our investment decisions, our money has a voice—use it wisely. It is a daily challenge, but if we're all making efforts, then collectively we can create meaningful change.

THE PROBLEM WITH FAST FOOD AND FAST MONEY

In 1949, Frank McNamara had dinner at Major's Cabin Grill in New York. The bill arrived and he realized he had forgotten his wallet. He worked his way around the problem and was inspired to come up with an alternative to cash. Soon after, he created the Diners Club Card, and by 1951 there were twenty thousand Diners Club cardholders. In 1959, American Express introduced the first card made of plastic, and by 1966 a national credit card system was formed and is now known as MasterCard. This is an interesting name, as I am sure the original intent was to allow people to be the master of

---

9   Food and Agriculture Organization of the United Nations, *Food Wastage Footprint: Impacts on Natural Resources*, 2013, http://www.fao.org/docrep/018/i3347e/i3347e. pdf.

their money. However, according to Consolidated Credit Counseling Services, Inc., the average credit card debt for households using credit cards is $15,799, with interest rates averaging 12.36 percent. In March 2012, the total revolving debt in the United States was $803.6 billion. The irony now is that plastic debt has become the master.

Around the same time, Richard and Maurice McDonald were establishing a small hamburger chain in California. As their success grew, others noticed and the idea of quick and easy eating establishments grew exponentially. In 1990, talk show host Johnny Carson labeled the hamburger the "McClog the Artery." We have all heard the health risks associated with the majority of fast food consumption. Obesity, diabetes, coronary disease, increased risk of stroke, and infections are just a few of the consequences of an unhealthy diet. According to the Food Research and Action Center, over one third of American adults are considered obese, as is one in six children.[10]

Here are the truths: we cannot borrow our way to prosperity, and we cannot indiscriminately eat our way to good health. What is the answer? Let's slow down! Mindfulness and intention around our eating and financial choices will help us live healthier, more fulfilling lives.

MONETARY MINDFULNESS

So much of our mind-set about money involves worrying about the future or rehashing our mistakes of the past. We are so consumed with how to make more of it, we let society entice and tempt us with how to spend it. We have our future calling us to task and our past

---

10   "Obesity in the US," FRAC, accessed June 9, 2017, http://frac.org/obesity-health/obesity-u-s.

admonishing our failures. If we can be mindful in the moment, for just a moment, we can open ourselves up to change.

Mindfulness is an amazing tool to help us understand ourselves by observing our thoughts, feelings, and physical sensations with an objective, nonjudgmental view. Once we acknowledge these components, we can look at what we want to do differently. In short, practicing monetary mindfulness helps us acknowledge and alter habitual behaviors by taking a moment to make different choices.

Many spiritual practices hold value in quiet contemplation, meditation, or centering prayer with a shift away from preoccupation with life circumstances and toward an appreciation of the moment and a greater perspective on life. Throughout history, this practice has been used to shift beliefs, attitudes, and behaviors toward the common good. Why not financial ones, too?

Professor Jon Kabat-Zinn of the University of Massachusetts Medical School is considered one of the founding fathers of modern mindfulness practices and has shown through scientific research how mindfulness contributes positively in a number of areas in our everyday lives, including:

1. Improves well-being by supporting attitudes that contribute to life satisfaction.

2. Helps us to be fully engaged in activities and gives us greater capacity to deal with adverse events.

3. Reduces our likelihood of getting caught up in worries about the future or regrets about the past.

4. Makes us less preoccupied with concerns about success and self-esteem and better able to form connections with others.

5.   Helps to improve physical health, relieve stress, lower blood pressure, and improve sleep.

6.   Improves mental health, decreases depression, and eases relational conflict.

Findings from a 2011 survey in *Journal of Happiness Studies* found that mindfulness:

1.   Strengthened immune system and physiological responses to stress and negative emotions.

2.   Improved social relationships with family and strangers.

3.   Reduced stress, depression, and anxiety to increase well-being and happiness.

4.   Increased openness to experience, conscientiousness, and agreeableness and reduced negative associations with neuroticism.

5.   Led to greater psychological mindfulness, which included an awareness that is clear, nonconceptual, and flexible; a practical stance toward reality; and present attention to the individual's consciousness and awareness.[11]

Cultivating monetary mindfulness is not easy to do. It will take time, but be patient and extend grace to yourself and others as you delve into this new world. We want to cram more and more into less and less time, and in doing so we lose sight of the damage that we are doing to ourselves. In the age of high-speed, digitized, instant everything, it is hard to slow down and equally hard to connect with our financial selves. There is a cultural taboo around slowing down,

---

11   Heidi A. Wayment, Bill Wiist, Bruce M. Sullivan, and Meghan A. Warren, "Doing and Being: Mindfulness, Health, and Quiet Ego Characteristics Among Buddhist Practitioners," *Journal of Happiness Studies* 12, no. 4 (2011): 575-589.

but we need to question what is not working and why. It's the only way we can discover the true value of what our money does for us and how we use it as a flow of our intentions.

Not only do we need to slow down with our financial decisions, but we need to look at how we set and work toward our goals.

LET'S BE SMART!

You have probably heard about "SMART" goals before, to create goals that are **specific**, **measurable**, **attainable**, **realistic**, and **tangible**. It can work, but for many, this formula for growth and goal setting can feel uninspiring or rigid, and they come up lacking because of it. Our quests become things we "should do" or "have to do," often based on deficiencies or cultural or societal expectations rather than personal ideals. But what if we looked at growth in our lives differently? Money Quotient*, an organization that develops Financial Life Planning* tools, has introduced a new play on SMART goals. What if we based goals or growth opportunities on whether they were significant, meaningful, attainable, rewarding, and timely?

We have to reimagine the world of personal finance in terms of daily financial health and long-term financial goals. Significant financial aspirations resonate with your soul. They keep you motivated and joyful as you move toward them, which means they have to be personalized to your values and priorities. Meaningful and attractive ambitions that have been painted with rich colors and clarity draw you toward them, making the sacrifices needed to accomplish them worthwhile. If your goals are rewarding, you use a different—perhaps bolder or more analytical—scale to weigh the costs of the commitment. You see the benefits not only for yourself but also as they extend to others. The day-to-day choices become clear as you honestly appraise the tensions that will exist. In other words, you're more determined to reach the goals because they matter to you in a much more prolific way.

We have seasons in our lives, so we want to properly address the timing of our endeavors. Some goals should have specific targets, and others should not. Life, after all, is about the continuum of progression and change, so how you facilitate successful transitions and growth opportunities (i.e., investments, divestments, career changes, education, etc.) depends on how willing you are to embrace them in the first place. Your circumstances and experiences are unique, and your response to change will be influenced greatly by them both. We all have an internal compass that reflects our values and priorities, but it can be thrown off course because of external pulls or circumstances outside of our control.

Are you satisfied that you are moving toward your personal financial benchmarks? Do you get caught up in the "finances are not my strength" or "I will deal with that stuff later" frame of mind? Do you compare how your investments are doing to the S&P 500 or the DOW without consideration of your objectives or your asset allocation? Mental obstacles and societal rhetoric need to be overcome. In the words of Henry Ford, "Obstacles are those frightful things you see when you take your eyes off your goal."

What area of your financial garden needs tending to during the summer season? It may be your charitable giving, your investment strategies, your tax management tactics, or your spending habits. It may be your level of financial education, feelings about your money life, or communication skills with those impacted by your decisions. Pick one area and decide how you want to improve or grow. Start there, building on your successes.

PERCEPTIONS OF WEALTH

A financial summer brings with it the surprising dilemma of having a **wealth conundrum**. A wealth conundrum forms when your financial life is bursting at the seams. Understandably, having too much money may not seem like much of a problem to many. Conversely, if you don't have a wealth conundrum, should you have one? Only you, as an individual, can really answer that question, but there are some clues and insights to help you find the answer.

Each of us needs to keep things in perspective. If you have change in your pocket, food in your fridge, a roof over your head, and clothing in your closet, you are in the top 10 percent of the world's wealth. We each need to wrestle with our personal perceptions of wealth regardless of our net worth. In doing so, I encourage you to dig deeper than what exists in your bank account.[12]

We are easily swayed, and deeply influenced, by our culture to believe that wealth is seen only through a financial lens. We're taught that more is better, that there is never enough, and that debt is normal just the way it is. What other types of wealth do we need to acknowledge and celebrate? There is the wealth found outdoors in nature. Wealth may be relational, found in rich connections with family and friends. Wealth may be realized in our physical health and mental capacities for being creative and resourceful or in the blessing of sharing our time, talent, and treasures with others. Wealth can be the peace found in contemplating a sunset or pursuing the opportunity to change the world. As your summer season unfolds, let your guiding question be this: What does true prosperity look like to me?

---

12 www.globalrichlist.com

How is your gratitude journal looking?

SHARPEN YOUR TOOLS

Even during a flourishing summer season, we often spend much of our time and energy focused on what we don't have instead of appreciating the abundance of everything we do have.

- Am I in charge of my money, or is my money in charge of me?

- How can the monetary mindfulness pie (10/10/10/70) help me take charge of my financial life?

- What is a SMART goal that I can set for this year?

- How do I define true prosperity?

How do you move toward healthy relationships with money that will enable you to build and sustain true financial and personal wealth in your life? It is a lifelong process, one that requires deep personal reflection, steadfast courage, inherent gratitude, transformational wisdom, and strategic implementation. Money, after all, should enhance your life's journey, not dictate it.

CHAPTER 8

NAVIGATING YOUR FINANCIAL TERRAIN

*The secret of change is to focus all your energy not
on fighting the old but on building the new.*

—SOCRATES, *WAY OF THE PEACEFUL
WARRIOR* BY DAN MILLMAN

We have all felt like a gerbil on the financial treadmill at one time
or another, just grinding away and seeing little improvement in
our financial health or our monetary mind-sets. We can blame the
economy, our circumstances, and even ourselves. Lack of progress
is frustrating, and it wears on you mentally, emotionally, and physically over time. Before long, it is all too easy to lose sight of, and lose
hope for, something different. The qualitative and quantitative com-

ponents of our wealth perspective can change. We can move from financially floundering to flourishing.

Noted psychologist and educator Dr. Martin Seligman presented "well-being theory" in his book *Authentic Happiness*. Seligman contends that individuals flourish in life when they experience five key elements: positive emotions, engagement, relationships, meaning, and accomplishment—all of which can be applied to your personal financial life and move you from frustration to fulfillment.

No matter what life or financial season you are in, it is vital to examine regularly the ways in which your resources can empower and mobilize you to live a fuller and more prosperous life. Seligman's well-being theory offers the perfect roadmap.

Past life satisfaction; present feelings of pleasure, happiness, joy, and comfort; and future feelings of optimism fall under the umbrella of **positive emotions**. What emotions are evoked when you think about your monetary life? What are some small steps you can take to improve those emotions? Again, more money only brings happiness up to a certain point. True financial health revolves around having positive feelings in how it comes to you, how you share it, how you are growing and protecting it, and how you spend it.

You can capitalize on positive financial emotions. For example, if you received a promotion or affirmation for your work, identify why you believe you were acknowledged. "I received a promotion at work because I put forth extra effort and I am good at what I do. It made me feel valued and competent in how I bring money in." Great! Now, apply those skills and your behavior to another area. "I am going to attend this conference because it will help me excel." If you have a positive emotion attached to a past experience, build on it. This would be a wise investment of your financial resources. Cultivating positive emotions around money no matter how much or how little you have is key. It is an outlook and an attitude that surpasses circumstances but can manifest through mindful intent.

Engagement is the feeling of being absorbed or immersed in a task or activity that uses your talents and strengths. Do you need to take classes, attend a workshop, or go to a conference that builds your strengths? Do you need to invest in your business, delve into a creative bent, or take a hobby to the next level? These decisions need to be made within the boundaries of your safe spending parameters, of course, but they are vital to your growth. Accumulating debt to try to find well-being will do just the opposite. Get creative and resourceful to avoid becoming stagnant.

Relationships encompass your experience with healthy, supportive, and meaningful people throughout your day. Your financial choices say much about your relationships, and simply by tracking your spending you will see which relationships you value the most. Money can also be used to manipulate relationships and create toxic environments. As such, you will likely find that you have amends to make or forgiveness to extend to get relationships back on track. You may also need to give additional responsibility without expectations to those who are ready to grow in their financial maturity, such as your children. If so, you should be preparing yourself to have difficult but necessary discussions in order to prepare them for receiving future financial responsibilities.

Meaning refers to your contributions to the world, knowing that you are an important part of something greater than yourself. Are your financial decisions strategic in this regard? Are you investing in experiences or creating margin in your work life in order to give back or do for others? Do you invest in companies that align with your values? Do you have a financial giving plan in place? Have you looked at financial tools such as donor-advised funds or charitable remainder trusts to leverage your giving? Take a proactive stance with your financial decisions instead of just reacting or letting life happen to you.

When you pursue mastery, giving it your best, knowing where you are supposed to be at any given moment, you embrace **accomplishment**. Accomplishment is realized financially when you have a clear vision of what true prosperity entails and your daily life reflects it. To realize a sense of accomplishment is a life of peace and bliss, standing at the stage we all seek for ourselves. A sense of accomplishment is not a destination, a goal attained, or an ending point. It is a culmination of daily financial choices in all the other areas previously noted. It is living life in true financial integrity.

The financial decisions you make to create positive emotions, engagement, relationships, meaning, and accomplishment infuse each other. It will take courage, and you will need to manage the tension innate in the process, but creating financial well-being will flow over and support you in the physical, relational, mental, and spiritual areas of your life as well. Revisit your "why" as a reminder and motivator to keep you moving forward. It will lead you to deliberate, consistent decisions in all areas of your financial life. Your "why" is the embodiment of your values, by which the standards for your behavior and judgment are set. Learning more about your values may inspire you to start a business or alter your career decisions. It may encourage you to invest in a product, service, or company or motivate you to donate more of your time and resources to a cause that resonates with your values. Your pocketbook follows your heart. Don't be afraid to search it!

SHARPEN YOUR TOOLS

As you seek well-being in your life and navigate the financial implications of creating life balance, consider the following questions:

- 🍂 What positive emotions around money do I want to cultivate?

- 🍂 How do I want to use my money to engage in life, creating satisfaction within safe bounds?

- 🍂 How are my relationships affected by my financial choices?

- 🍂 What do my finances say about what is important to me?

- 🍂 What do I want my money story, told at the end of my life, to be?

CHAPTER 9

WHAT RISK ARE YOU WILLING TO TAKE?

Our greatest weakness lies in giving up. The most certain way to succeed is always to try just one more time.

—THOMAS A. EDISON

Over twenty years ago, our youngest child starting skiing. We lovingly equipped her with a colorful locally made ski suit, tiny skis, and a helmet that made her look like a bobblehead. My husband bought his helmet, and I scoffed, "One more thing to buy. I've grown up skiing without one. I don't need or want one." I rationalized that I was a conservative skier. "I don't go bashing through the trees," I thought. "A helmet will mat my hair worse than a hat, and I won't be able to hear." My excuses went on. I was willing to accept the risk that I would not sustain a head injury while skiing, despite the very real chance that I could or would.

We live in a world full of risk, and the financial implications of risk are always close behind. There are financial consequences if we die prematurely, have health issues, or even live too long. There are monetary implications connected to the risk of investing or not investing.

We can retain, avoid, reduce, share, or transfer financial risk in a variety of ways. We all understand the harmful effects of financial loss. Friends and families, communities, and even strangers often help each other out when a financial need arises as a result of unmitigated risk. There is an intrinsic, deep-rooted, genuine societal value to serving and allowing ourselves to be assisted. Nonetheless, what portion of financial risk in our personal lives should we be accountable for? We can start by taking responsibility for how we invest.

TYPES OF RISK AND HOW TO MANAGE THEM

In my ideal investment world, everyone would get a high rate of return, complete safety, and immediate liquidity. There would be no taxes on yield or growth and we could just invest, forget about it, and enjoy life. But my ideal world doesn't exist (hence giving me job security), so one of the first steps in understanding the "real financial world" needs to be acknowledging the different types of risk and deciding how to handle them. This will help you manage the certainty of uncertainty.

Most people are familiar with **market risk**. This is the possibility of downward changes in the market price of an investment. To help manage market risk, you need a strategy. You want to develop a strategy based on your goals, your age, and the different assets you have available to tap into for different seasons of life. An *investment policy statement* defines why you are investing and what risk you are willing to take for each of your investment "buckets." Within each different bucket of investments, you want to asset allocate based on your stomach for volatility and to rebalance your portfolio periodically. You will also want to look at whether the current economic environment favors an active or passive investment strategy. An active strategy is where you have investment managers making decisions about the underlying investment holdings. A passive strategy is where you "buy and hold." There is no perfect "recipe," and you want to understand the underlying reasons and costs associated with what will best serve you.

We also have **inflationary risk**. With tools and strategies that provide safety from market risk, such as savings accounts, CDs, T-bills, and stashing cash under the mattress, you will have your dollars, but they will buy less and less over time. We will see inflation; the price of a loaf of bread and the cost of health care will go up over time. Setting aside money consistently for future use in appropriately asset allocated "buckets," sheltered from current taxes as applicable, and rebalanced as warranted are all viable strategies to keep you ahead of inflation risk.

There are several other types of investment risk that require a case-by-case assessment of factors, including **credit** or **default risk**, **liquidity risk,** and **interest rate risk**, as well as the possibility of tax law changes. There will always be risk with any investment, but by evaluating your investments from as many angles as possible, you can mitigate and manage the associated risk.

There is an assortment of financial products and techniques that can help you manage risk, too. Life, health, and disability insurances, annuities, principal-protected mutual fund products, diversification, and tactical wealth management have all been created to help you mollify risk. Educate yourself on the vehicles that will give you peace of mind in managing financial uncertainty, but be cautious about letting fear drive your decisions. There are unscrupulous salespeople out there who feed on your fears with inappropriate or overly complicated products. Come up with your plan first, then the product. Make sure you're not being hardheaded or dismissive about the potential for risk.

One of the biggest risks we have in pursuing our goals is ourselves. We can be our own worst enemies when it comes to investment or financial decisions. Jason Zweig, in his book *Your Money and Your Brain*, unpacks many lessons from the field of neuroeconomics. The brain chemicals released when we look at our statement and see large gains or have a financial "win"—adrenaline and dopamine—are the same ones released when a person is high on cocaine. The overall effect plays into "greed" and keeps us seeking out the sensation of elation, which is usually unsustainable. It would make sense to stay on a sensible, reasonable financial growth path, but in our brain, getting what we planned on is a nonevent. Because of brain chemistry, we need increasingly bigger hits of adrenaline or dopamine to get the same feeling over time. When we have a financial loss, it registers in the same area of the brain wired to respond to mortal danger. Financial losses hurt much more than gains feel good. This creates what is called "loss aversion." We sell at the worst time, or we fear getting back in the market. This is a huge barrier to our long-term financial health. Recognizing that our brains don't work well on money is the first step in managing the emotions that can work against us. The next step is to give thoughtful consideration to how to manage the different types of risk out there.

ASSESSING YOUR RISK TOLERANCE

The Roaring Fork Valley in my native Colorado attracts risk takers with a range of type A personalities, outdoor enthusiasts, and business entrepreneurs. In my early days here, I excitedly jumped over the edge of Walsh's ski run on Aspen Mountain and kayaked the Slaughterhouse run on Roaring Fork River without any thought of the risk I was taking and the possible painful consequences or long-term effects of my endeavors. Now, I look at risk differently, especially in my vocational calling. In the world of setting life goals and handling money, how do we correctly assess and manage our market investment risk?

The industry standard for evaluating investment **risk tolerance** can range from a few short questions to several pages of inquiry around your financial and emotional ability to tolerate market fluctuations. With questions answered, a "suitability" is determined that incorporates your attitudes about risk, your time horizon, your need for income, and your other available assets, and an investment portfolio is designed for implementation. This portfolio is not to be a complete picture, however, and it should not be used as the only gauge for determining an investment strategy.

The problem with the traditional approach is that it confuses someone's capacity to expose themselves to volatility with their actual need or desire to do so. To more accurately determine your "risk tolerance," you need to quantify several aspects of your goals. True speculation capacity is a measure of how risky your goals are. For example, does the goal you are working toward *require* a high rate of return just to have a chance of success, or does the goal have such a low level of exposure that even a bad market can't derail it?

A risk tolerance questionnaire is a great place to start but a lousy place to stop. Dig deeper and qualify, prioritize, and quantify meaningful life goals. The optimal investment strategy needs to incorporate the portfolio you are considering and the goals that you are aiming to achieve. It is crucial that neither the portfolio nor the goal is exposed to more volatility than what you can actually tolerate. A planner who adheres to the "fiduciary standard" (looking out for your best interest) will walk alongside you in a different capacity than an advisor who is only determining if a product is suitable for you. Everyone is tolerant and accepting of risk when there isn't any. When market conditions are somewhat stable and moving in an upward momentum, everyone is comfortable. But when it starts getting precarious, most investors have little risk tolerance. In the end, emotions take over and they capitulate to selling in a down market. Knowing yourself and your stomach for roller coaster rides, as well as understanding market risk itself, will help you ascertain positioning for the optimal investment outcome.

Once you understand and embrace your need for and capacity for market fluctuations, you can use financial metrics such as standard deviation to evaluate your portfolio options. Standard deviation is a quantification of how much a return can deviate from the mean. The higher the number, the more volatile the investment or portfolio is. Stocks will have a higher standard deviation than bonds. Some may feel that their risk tolerance is associated with age and that a younger investor can have a portfolio with a higher standard deviation than a person nearing retirement can. "You're younger. You're going to be in the market for years, so you have time to recover . . ." But that line of logic isn't necessarily true. For a young person who is a good saver and has reasonable goals set for the future, they may be very comfortable going slow and steady and not riding the emotional and market roller coaster.

While there isn't a perfect investment out there, there are many ways to create wealth strategically. Before you invest in anything, however, you should ask yourself a number of important questions, such as: Why am I investing? Do I have adequate savings to tap into in the event of an emergency? How long before I need this money? What season is the economy in? What life season am I in? What are the potential tax implications of this investment? Are there investments I want to stay away from or support as a matter of principal?

If you have invested in companies that you believe in, whether it's their corporate governance, the product they produce, or the service they offer, you'll be more willing to stick with them when an economic season goes up and down. If the only reason you're investing is to hit a 10 percent rate of return, you will end up chasing returns, changing advisors, and hurting yourself in the long run.

Back on the slopes of Aspen, while I initially felt good about and vocally justified my decision not to wear a ski helmet, a bit of time and processing (and some pressure from those I skied with) shifted my perspective. My husband bought me a comfortable, safe brain bucket and I have worn it dutifully ever since. I suggest you take a look at different areas of risk in your own life and determine how you want to manage them.

SHARPEN YOUR TOOLS

Like life, finance is full of risk. It's impossible to predict when, where, and how it will manifest in your financial life, but you can work to minimize your exposure to it and its costs.

- ✒ Who will be affected by your decisions to take on various types of risk, and what would be the financial impact on those you care about?

ø Does your asset allocation strategy align with your risk capacity as well as your risk tolerance?

ø What insurances do you have in place, and are they still working for you properly?

ø Have you experienced any life transitions that warrant looking at the type of risk you are exposed to?

CHAPTER 10

SHARING THE BOUNTY

*It is more difficult to give money away intelligently
than to earn it in the first place.*

—ANDREW CARNEGIE

It is inherently beneficial to help improve the human condition by being a part of something bigger than ourselves. As Winston Churchill once said, "We make a living by what we get, but we make a life by what we give." Christ understood the benefit, too, telling his followers that "it is more blessed to give than to receive." A new season is upon us and blooming with new ways of doing money. How we earn, give, nurture, protect, and spend is quickly changing. Conscious consumerism, angel philanthropy, impact investing, and the sharing economy have taken root, grabbing people's attention and intention. We are now creating new wealth, in new ways. What will be different as we embrace these opportunities given the timeless, fertile soil of kindness?

The flowers of generosity are perennial. We saw it played out through the recession, as Americans banded together to help one another out, as well as others around the world. Whether it was symptomatic of empathy due to personal loss or sympathy from those who were less affected and felt compelled to help, the amount of charity within the United States jumped. A 2014 survey from the Corporation for National and Community Service (CNCS) and the National Conference on Citizenship (NCoC), for instance, found that roughly one in four Americans volunteered with an organization, more than ever before, and that three out of every five Americans reported informal volunteering by providing labor or financial help to their neighbors, friends, family, or strangers.[13] Citizens of this great nation are givers. Since 2002, Americans have donated 104.9 billion hours of help to others, a number the NCoC values at approximately $2.1 trillion in labor costs.

With technology, we are better connected and more informed. Building on compassion, we can be proactive in how we engage and make our philanthropic decisions. Let's cultivate the soil of giving with guts and gratitude.

As your summer season continues to produce the fruits of your labor, and as your wealth continues to grow from proper planning and preparation, you can be strategic and thoughtful in how you want to share your bounty.

---

13   "New Report: 1 in 4 Americans Volunteer; 3 in 5 Help Neighbors," Corporation for National and Community Service website, posted December 8, 2015, https://www.nationalservice.gov/newsroom/press-releases/2015/new-report-1-4-americans-volunteer-3-5-help-neighbors.

APPRECIATION BEGETS APPRECIATION

There are two ways to look at appreciation—the **qualitative** and **quantitative**. The qualitative element of appreciation refers to the feelings of gratitude for one's resources and circumstances. Studies have shown that the appreciative mind-set will likely be the best predictor of increasing wealth and well-being in your life.

COMPONENTS OF APPRECIATION

Qualitative—Your feelings of gratitude

Quantitative—How are your assets growing?

In *The Soul of Money,* Lynne Twist writes that appreciative thinking is the opposite of scarcity thinking: "When your attention is on what's lacking and scarce—in your life, in your work, in your family, in your town—then that becomes what you are about." If however, you focus on gratitude and abundance, "The happiest and most joyful people I know are those who express themselves through channeling their resources—money, when they have it—on to their highest commitments. Theirs is a world where the experience of wealth is in sharing what they have, giving, allocating, and expressing themselves authentically with the money they put in flow."

The quantitative element of appreciation encompasses the increasing value of your financial assets. The beauty of diversification is that different assets will appreciate at different rates at different times for different reasons. Keep an eye on your total net worth and make sure your liabilities are decreasing. You need to reconnect with what you have, ascertaining what changes need to be made given your current situation and your overall goals. This may be assessing the equity in your home or the allocation strategy within your retirement accounts, or it may be delving into the profitability of your business assets. Why do you have them? What are they doing for you and for others? What changes need to be made?

SPONTANEOUS AND PLANNED GIVING

Once you connect the qualitative and quantitative components of appreciation in your life, you can look at two types of giving—**systematic giving** and **symptomatic giving**.

Systematic giving, like its name suggests, is when you have a plan and know how much you are giving on a monthly basis. This is the bread and butter of what nonprofits need. They crave sustainability for their programs and means for reasonable growth. When they have sustainable, assured sources of income in place, their time can be focused on programs, not fundraising.

Symptomatic giving is spontaneous—it's what happens when a need arises and, with a click of your mouse, a text from your phone, or the push of a button, you share your financial resources. It is the heartstring appeal, and huge amounts of money can be raised quickly using this method. Take, for example, the fundraising efforts following the wildfire tragedy in Gatlinburg, Tennessee, in 2016. The fires claimed fourteen lives, destroyed more than 2,400 structures, and turned more than seventeen thousand acres of forest into char. The area's most famous resident, Dolly Parton, quickly organized a telethon to raise money for both the victims and the tourist-dependent town, and within a matter of hours more than $9 million had been donated to the relief fund.[14] Perhaps one of the largest examples

---

14   Andrew Weil and Melissa Erickson, "$9 million raised for Dolly Parton's 'My People Fund' so far," WBIR website, December 15, 2016, http://www.wbir.com/news/local/

of symptomatic giving occurred after a series of tsunamis struck a number of coastal countries in South and Southeast Asia in 2004. More than 228,000 lives were lost, two million were left homeless, and billions of dollars' worth of damage was incurred as a result of the disaster. Donations poured in from around the globe, and by the end of the year, $6.25 billion in financial aid had been raised.[15] In the words of Margaret Mead, "Never doubt that a small group of thoughtful, committed citizens can change the world; indeed, it's the only thing that ever has."

The world needs both types of contributions, and we all get the opportunity to share what we have. A powerful way to foster healthy giving habits is to know what you have, decide how much is enough for yourself and your family, and then make intentional decisions on what, where, how, and why you want to give.

YOUR GIVING STRATEGY

Philanthropic opportunities are prolific and perennial. There are invites to fundraisers, paper petitions for end-of-year gifts, phone calls explaining enticing programs, and touching commercials and billboards streaming into our lives from every direction. Do we give to our place of worship, local nonprofits, international NGOs? There are so many good causes and wonderful organizations that it's challenging to decide. What best aligns with your values, interests, and convictions?

While my husband and I give more than some and less than others—we enjoy giving. We have embraced it as part of having a

smoky-mountains-rise-a-benefit-for-the-my-people-fund/369608052.

15   Carla Kweifio-Okai, "Where Did the Indian Ocean Tsunami Aid Money Go?" *The Guardian*, December 25, 2014.

healthy relationship with money. We challenge ourselves to step out of our comfort zone. When we give, we acknowledge our blessings and the opportunities to share with others. We have never found ourselves "wanting" and embrace contentment as a gift in and of itself. This mind-set has been a journey for us, one that continues with twists and turns, conversations and commitments, faith and freedoms. As Maya Angelou said, "I have found that among its other benefits, giving liberates the soul of the giver."

As a financial advisor, it is my job to understand timely tools and techniques and walk alongside clients to explore and expand their philanthropic journey. Here are some things to consider as you decide what your giving strategy should entail.

Why do you give? There are a variety of reasons why you might want to donate your time and/or money. Learning what your reasons are will help you make better choices in how you give. For instance, do you want to make a difference? Are you passionate about a cause? Do you want to live in integrity with your faith or spiritual values? Do you want to simplify your life? Do you want to create a living legacy? Like most areas of your financial journey, the "why" needs to come first in plans for giving and should be discussed with those who are impacted by your financial decisions. You want relational alignment as you gain traction in giving. The "why" may change depending on what season of life you are in and as you improve the condition of your financial health.

The next thing you need to consider is how much of your spending plan should be systematic or symptomatic giving. Jason Franklin, the executive director of Bolder Giving, recommends the 50/30/20 idea; that is, 50 percent of your giving plan is focused on one charity—the one cared about the most—and 30 percent is targeted for causes and organizations that you want to support on a monthly basis (systematic). Finally, 20 percent is reserved for small impulse gifts (symptomatic). These are the opportunities for random acts of kindness, or to be part of a social networking appeal when warranted. Ron Blue, a thought leader in the Christian financial world, suggests giving 10 percent of your income at your place of worship as a place to start but not a place to stop. The main goal is to get strategic with your giving. This will keep you focused on what is important to you and free you from the guilt about not giving to everyone who makes an appeal.

What do you give? You can simply write a check or click for a cause that is always dollar-for-dollar giving. You can get more leverage when you give appreciated assets, investment assets such as stocks, bonds, and mutual funds, or even shares of privately held businesses, real estate, or more complex assets. However, the receiving organization needs to be set up to receive and facilitate a sale if necessary. You can work around that by using a **donor-advised fund (DAF)**. With a DAF, charitable contributions can be made with cash, appreciated assets, or other complex gifts and receive an immediate tax benefit. You and your family can then make recommendations for disbursements (grants) to organizations over time.

You can also make beneficiary designations on life insurance policies, annuities, and personal or employer-sponsored retirement plans. With many of these contractual designations, you need to have spousal consent if you are married.

For 2017, the annual gift exclusion is $14,000. This means you can give away $14,000 to anybody you want without having to file a gift tax return. If you are married, you can each give away $14,000. Tax laws will continue to evolve based on politics and policy, but right now the gift tax exemption is $5.49 million per individual. No federal estate or gift tax would be due. Most people don't know that you can give this amount away while you are living instead of transferring on death. Do you want to do your giving while you're living so that you know where it goes? How do you determine how much is needed for yourself and others under your care so that you can release your financial power to impact the world—one dollar at a time?

How do you give? As mentioned, a DAF is a philanthropic vehicle that is, next to cash giving, the easiest to drive. The sponsoring organization (i.e., the DAF) is a 501(c)(3) and does all the due diligence on grants and record keeping. The tax deductions are up to 50 percent of adjusted gross income for giving cash and up to 30 percent of AGI for donating appreciated assets to the fund. Donors can avoid capital gains on contributions of appreciated assets and receive immediate fair market value tax deductions.

Once the donation has been made to the DAF, you have shifted ownership of the assets, but you still have several elements of control. You can make donations either anonymously or in your name. You will not receive an additional tax deduction from the charitable organization you are giving to, because you already gave it to the DAF sponsor. Once you make a donation—either of cash or appreciated assets—everything is moved into cash. You can keep it all in cash, or you can invest in an appropriate asset allocation model. You decide when and how to distribute the proceeds, how often, and to whom. It can be done all at once, or you can spread it out over time. A DAF is a great way to bring your family together around the giving conversation. You can name children or others as the future grant makers of the DAF.

There are some challenges within the DAF world. DAF sponsors are becoming the country's largest charitable entities. Since there are not distribution requirements like those found in private foundations, people can just let the money in the DAF sit and not distribute anything to organizations.[16] The only ones who benefit then are the financial institutions and managers. If you are going to use the tool, use it for its intended purpose and keep the money flowing to causes and concerns you deem important.

What financial tool is the best fit for your philanthropic intentions?

Another widely used tool for philanthropic purposes is the **charitable remainder trust (CRT)**. This is a legal, irrevocable trust that is set up to receive assets, such as cash, appreciated investments, real estate, etc. Unlike the DAF, where you do not receive any income benefit from the vehicle, a CRT is set up to give you—and possibly other family members—income for a period of time. At the end of this period, the remainder goes to the charitable organization of your choosing. There are tax benefits to the CRT, but they are much more complex than those of the DAF and direct contributions. The tax deduction is based on the current value of the charity's benefit in receiving the assets at some time in the future, taking three factors into account:

1. The estimated length of time the charity must wait to receive the funds.

2. What percentage of the trust will be going to the income beneficiaries and the frequency of that payment (annually or monthly). Usually, the rate will be between 5 and 7

---

16 Peter J. Reilly, "Donor-Advised Funds: The Good, the Bad and the Ugly," *Forbes*, June 24, 2016, http://www.forbes.com/sites/peterjreilly/2016/06/24/donor-advised-funds-the-good-the-bad-and-the-ugly/#322a04f16029.

percent. The higher the rate, the less will be available for the beneficiary organization, so the smaller the tax deduction.

3. The current investment return on the assets held inside the trust.

Where do you give? Once you narrow down your heart direction, how do you vet the multitude of organizations that petition for your financial attention? An easy answer is to give to a charity or organization close to where you live that you know already does good work. If you don't know of a good charity or would like to learn more about one you have in mind, you can find several websites dedicated to evaluating charities from a variety of perspectives, including GreatNonprofits.org, MyPhilanthropedia.org, and Ministrywatch.com.

Sharing your financial resources is only one approach to giving. Becoming directly involved in the projects and causes you're donating to is sometimes hard to do but can be even more rewarding. Again, this may vary based on the season of life you are in. You are a vital part of the change you want to see in the world. Commit to prioritizing time to share your expertise and talent with organizations that need your participation.

RESERVATIONS ABOUT GIVING MORE?

In order to give with guts and gratitude, reflect on what may be holding you back:

- I don't feel secure enough in how much I have.

- I don't know what could be considered "surplus."

- I'm too busy.

- I have conflicting values about giving—within myself or among family members.

- I've been discouraged in the past around accountability issues.

- I've been discouraged about making real, meaningful change in the world.

- I'm preserving money for children, grandchildren, or other family members.

- I'm waiting for the right cause or moment to come along.

- I'm afraid of making mistakes I'll regret.

Don't capitulate to any of these defenses. Press into and through them, coming out the other side with insight and intent and embracing the beauty and benefits of this crucial component of financial health and well-being.

WHEN HELPING HURTS

While it is never our intent, sometimes giving can hurt. Whether to family or organizations, we don't want our financial decisions to keep people from reaching their full potential.

New insight into philanthropic giving is providing a stark picture of what has gone wrong in helping. Humanitarian giving when a disaster strikes is different, of course. We need to respond and we need to respond quickly. People need immediate assistance, and our help can be the difference between a person having basic needs such as safety, food, clothing, and shelter or not.

But when it comes to charitable giving, the path to what is helpful and what is not is much less clear. As the proverb goes, "Give a man a fish and he'll eat for a day. Teach a man to fish and he'll eat for a lifetime." Knowing exactly how to distinguish between a hand up and a handout is something we all need to wrestle with. Our hearts are in the right place, but we need to really look around and discern what the overall impact might be from our giving. When we give a person a fish, or clothing, or shoes, could it be that we are doing them and others harm? There may be local fishermen, tailors, or cobblers that are providing services or items for sale, for example. When given the option of getting something for free or paying for a good or service, which would you choose?

I saw this in Tanzania, Africa. There were piles (like garbage mounds) of used clothing sent from First World countries that people could pick through. And pick they did. Everywhere, we saw people wearing T-shirts, shorts, ball caps, and dresses emblazoned with sports logos and insignias from the United States.

Comically, we found ourselves in "need" of warmer jackets. We were lead to a row of small clothing shops that had clean sweaters, jackets, and pants pleasantly displayed. These entrepreneurs had gone through the piles of First World cast-off clothing, picked out the better quality items, cleaned them up, and put them out for sale. I found it humorous that we traveled halfway around the world to purchase clothing that we had given away at home! These shop owners were providing a value-added service to people who didn't want to pick through the piles. They were compensated for their efforts, building self-esteem while knowing they were contributing to their economies.

But there is also a shadow side to the free clothing, footwear, or other well-meaning intents of First World countries. In Tanzania's case, there was "too much" free clothing available. There wasn't much need for a start-to-finish marketplace, as growing the cotton, shearing the wool, creating the fabrics, and making, distributing, and retailing the clothing were all made unnecessary. The proliferation of free clothing piles was suffocating local businesses. For this community, it meant fewer jobs, fewer entrepreneurial endeavors, and ultimately, the denial of a person's ability to provide for themselves and their families with dignity.

Aid doesn't help countries become sustainably financially healthy, but trade does. Educating and empowering people to obtain skills to contribute, to build, and to create a life of meaning and purpose is the greatest thing you can give.

As you enjoy your summer financial season, take the time to discuss giving as often as you discuss building wealth. They go hand in hand and are both essential parts of living a healthy financial life! Connect with what is holding you back, dig into strategic ways to give, and take the time to learn what impact your giving has on others. You may be inspired and satisfied, or you may discover that your giving, while heartfelt, has unintended, negative impact and needs to be realigned. It is well worth the efforts.

In order to experience true beauty throughout your financial journey in each of its unique seasons, let the qualitative element of appreciation be your guide. Appreciation as an attitude toward life leads to contentment. Espousing contentment will release you from a mind-set of scarcity to cultivate an outlook of abundance. This abundance will be made manifest in the appreciation of your financial resources, which you can release to the world with an "investment" in promoting human dignity. Are you ready to climb on board?

SHARPEN YOUR TOOLS

You want to align your pocketbook with your passions. If you don't, you will eventually grow discontented with and disconnected from your money. As you create your giving plan, start with a few basic questions:

- 🖋 What motivates you to explore your giving potential? Which of these statements best describes you (select all that apply):

  Impact—I want to make the biggest difference I can.

  Passion for a cause—There's a specific cause or concern I want to help with.

  Faith—I want to live in harmony with my religious or spiritual values.

  Fairness—I want to share with the greater community.

  Simplicity—I have enough; giving it away simplifies my life.

  Satisfaction—It gives me great joy and meaning to give of my resources.

- 🖋 Do you feel content with your life?

- 🖋 Does your current giving align with your passion, your purpose, and who you are as a giver?

- 🖋 What needs to happen to create additional capacity with your financial resources, your time, or the ability to share your talents?

FALL: DISTRIBUTION

As summer ebbs into fall, we embrace the changes that happen both in life and in our finances. The fall life season has traditionally been seen as "midlife," ranging from age fifty to seventy. This may include leaving a career or addressing waning physical issues. A financial "fall" (harvesting what has been set aside), however, may occur within any of your personal life seasons. For example, you may need to dig into savings to invest in the "spring" of a business venture, or you may want to uncover the tax implications of taking money out of your IRA to fund a child's education as you move through your "summer." Financial harvesting involves understanding how your assets and liabilities are working (or not) as you decide how to access them. It encompasses a very different scope and complexity of issues than you faced in your financial summer "accumulation" season.

CHAPTER 11

THE ECOSYSTEM OF YOUR FINANCIAL LIFE

Growth is never by mere chance; it is the
result of forces working together.

—JAMES CASH

An ecosystem in nature is the interaction of living organisms with the nonliving components of their environment. A healthy natural ecosystem is where these elements work well together for the benefit of the whole system. You can look at the ecosystem of your financial life as the complex interaction that includes—but is not limited to— your personal genetic predispositions, your personality, your financial and personal assets and liabilities, and the interaction with economic, geopolitical, and market environments as you pass through each of your personal life seasons. Needless to say, your financial ecosystem is extremely complex, it is never static, and it requires monitoring and modifications to optimize how it functions.

What are the components of your life balance sheet? A financial ledger consists of assets and liabilities. Strange as it may sound, the same can be said of our life. Looking closely at our assets and liabilities will often reveal as many hidden dangers as untapped resources.

ON ONE SIDE OF THE LEDGER: ASSETS

A broad definition of an asset is anything that is, or could be, serving you and is expected to grow in value over time. It may be tangible and monetarily calculable, such as a home, rental property, a vintage car, or a rare collector's item. An asset may also be something more abstract whose real market value is indeterminable, such as relationships or character traits. Friendships, for instance, can be great assets. If you have a partner who is supportive, encouraging, and helps you to be a better version of yourself at work, at home, and beyond, that's a priceless asset!

WHAT DO YOU CONSIDER TO BE YOUR MOST VALUABLE ASSETS?

Proverbs 16:16 extols, "How much better to get wisdom than gold, to get insight rather than silver!" Are you creative, resilient, resourceful? Are you growing in wisdom and discernment? Your most valuable assets are not necessarily your material possessions. Spend some time pondering your assets; you may discover new opportunities and resources useful to your financial goals you never knew you had.

Your financial assets and economic wealth consists of four distinct components: *human capital, pension wealth, real estate wealth,* and *financial capital.* It's important to note that the relative weight of these units will change as you move through your financial life seasons addressing risk, volatility, and impact on your family.

Human capital is your working capacity, which obviously holds a high relative weight in your younger years and diminishes as you move toward retirement. Unfortunately, many people don't connect their ability to work to their human capital. Instead, they develop a mind-set that tells them, "Yeah. I have a job that I have to do. I go to it every day and that's it." Your ability to work, however, is an invaluable asset that needs to be managed wisely. If you are not maximizing your human capital now, then you are missing out on future wealth creation.

How do you bring money into your life with dignity, competency, integrity, grace, and joy?

How do your character traits fit into the asset category of human capital? Are you creative? Are you determined, loyal, and disciplined? Are you kind, ambitious, cooperative, optimistic? How do you build on and leverage positive character assets to increase your human capital? In the same way that we want to have a positive balance sheet, we want to make sure we're utilizing our assets, whether economic or character assets, in ways that move us in a direction of financial health and wealth creation.

If you are fortunate to love what you do for a living, your human capital may continue to have positive value throughout most of your life. We can observe that someone who has more positive character traits generally enjoys his or her job, is more likely to have a savings account, is in better physical health, and typically employs a variety of different buckets of financial net worth to serve them in different ways. On the other hand, someone who is really negative about life is generally unsatisfied with his or her job, is more likely to be in credit card debt, tends to be less concerned about his or her physical health, and usually has very few, if any, financial buckets in place to serve them.[17]

The next three wealth components will have low relative weights early on, but they each have the potential to grow over time. Your **pension wealth** may be Social Security, a state-sponsored plan, or a corporate program that will provide you with a future systematic payout. If you participate in a pension program, it is important to understand how it works in tandem with your other buckets.

Real estate wealth is an asset that, for many, will increase in market value over time as well as build equity as you pay down mortgages. Unfortunately, many tend to "sell one room away at a time" as they continuously refinance to pay off consumer credit card debt. Real estate wealth may be in the form of your primary residence or investment properties and can be utilized in a variety of ways for distribution and legacy planning.

---

17 Senad Karavdic and Michele Baumann, "Positive Career Attitudes Effect on Happiness and Life Satisfaction by Master Students and Graduates," *Open Journal of Social Sciences* 2014, no. 2, 15-23.

Finally, your **financial capital** is the money you have in a variety of vehicles inclusive of your savings accounts, IRAs, 401(k)s, trusts, and brokerage accounts. These assets, while usually more liquid than pension or real estate wealth, need to be managed judiciously based on your needs for liquidity today and spending needs for tomorrow.

Economic wealth comprises these four facets and changes as our societal norms evolve. It is rare to see a person go to school, head into a career, work for the same company for forty-five years, and retire with a pension, as was common with the "Greatest Generation," the parents of the baby boomers. Defined benefit programs have become a minor part of pension wealth as defined contribution plans (401(k), SEP, SIMPLE plans) have taken over. Studies show that millennials are less likely to purchase and hold primary real estate as compared to previous generations, as their lives have become more transient around work.[18] This fluidity of personal economic wealth needs to be intentionally and strategically managed as the economic, societal, and personal seasons of life ebb and flow.

As you look at your work capacity, your pension wealth and your real estate wealth, alongside your financial (investment) capital, should you manage the investment component to mitigate risk differently? Customary asset management looks at reducing volatility and risk management through diversification, asset allocation, hedging, or other traditional practices. Morningstar's David Blanchett and Philip Straehl's piece "No Portfolio Is an Island" posits that we need to look at a household's total economic wealth in tandem to come up with a true picture for managing volatility, portfolio design, and life stage implementation.

---

18   Diana Olick, "Millennials Cause Homeownership Rate to Drop to Lowest Level Since 1965," Realty Check, CNBC.com, July 28, 2016.

An example of how not considering a family's total economic wealth picture played out detrimentally in my region of central Colorado during the recession. It was a perfect storm for real estate agents who were winding down their human capital contribution to their wealth in 2007 and 2008. Many had put all their financial eggs in the sector they knew best—real estate. Compound this heavy sector weighting with their timing of retirement and their exposure to financial risk increased dramatically. Their Social Security or defined benefit program may have been stable, but if investment assets also included real estate investment trusts (REITS) as an "alternative investment" of a diversified portfolio, then real estate overweighted three areas of their economic wealth, and the recession wreaked havoc on their lives. Risk management needs to look at your financial picture holistically, taking into account all four spheres of economic wealth and how to proactively manage the opportunities and risks inherent at different life stages

We can let fear or greed throw the financial capital portion of our financial lives out of whack if we are not mindful, acting like lemmings and following the herd. We pay too much attention to what the talking heads say in the media and how our investment portfolios are doing compared to "benchmarks." We emotionally put too much weight on the financial capital portion when in reality it is only a piece of our comprehensive wealth management program. When you review your overall financial picture, make sure to include all four pieces of your economic wealth (human capital, pensions, real estate, and other financial) along with your flourishing character trait assets.

THE OTHER SIDE OF THE LEDGER: LIABILITIES

Along with your economic assets comes a host of liabilities. There are **balance sheet liabilities,** such as home mortgage, credit card debt, a car loan, or **business liabilities**. To put it bluntly, if you owe people money, you have a liability. These types of liabilities work against us, weighing us down financially and putting us at risk given personal and economic uncertainties that exist.

Just as we looked at the human capital character trait assets, there are also character trait liabilities. If you are in debt or working a job you are not thriving at, it impacts your outlook on life, net worth, and self-worth. And if you are lazy, difficult to work with (e.g., argumentative, arrogant, selfish, dishonest, etc.), or just no fun to be around, the value of your human capital is dramatically reduced, even jeopardized entirely if your traits are so bad that employers or colleagues decide that you're intolerable.

YOU CAN CHANGE

Positive and negative traits may be innate but can also be built upon or cultivated, recognized, and revamped. What personal reflection and work do you want to undertake to build on your positive character traits or capture and extinguish the negative ones? It is worth the effort and investment to increase your human capital capacity.

If you are already aware of your poor traits and are working to repair bad spending habits or a dissatisfied work life, then you may find inspiration in the words of famed psychologist and neurologist Viktor Frankl:

"When we are no longer able to change a situation, we are challenged to change ourselves. . . . Between stimulus and response there is a space. In that space is our power to choose our response. In our response lies our growth and our freedom."

Just because you may have been a certain way for thirty years doesn't mean you have to stay that way. You have created habits, and you can create new ones. Scientists now know that you can actually change the neural pathways in your brain to do things differently.

By saying that you're a victim of misfortune, that the world dealt you an unfair hand and there's nothing you can do about it, you are essentially "training" your brain to believe you don't have control over your life or your choices. Once you settle into that mind-set, life is just happening *to* you rather than *for* you. Before long, whatever choices, skills, blessings, or opportunities you do have fade out of sight. No matter how out of control your life may feel, there are many things you do have control over every single day, not the least of which is your attitude.

Science now shows that if we take the initiative to practice positive character traits, over time we can alter the way our brain responds to certain stimuli. In other words, by choosing to think positive thoughts, your brain will actually begin to "think" more positively for you. Once it does, engaging in better habits and behaviors is progressively easier to do because it's met with an increasingly diminished resistance to the change. That means that just by being more conscious about your actions and the thoughts that inform them, you might drastically improve your physical health, your relationships, your work experience, your economic wealth. Life as you know it may be transformed simply by adopting a better attitude! Maybe moms everywhere were right to tell us when we needed an "attitude adjustment" or to "turn that frown upside down." As it turns out, it's one of our most valuable and enduring assets.

SHARPEN YOUR TOOLS

As you work through financial and life seasons, it is important to understand the complexity of components that make up your financial ecosystem. As in nature, you want your financial ecosystems to thrive. What do you want to build on or change in yours?

- What are your current "tangible" assets (real estate, investments, retirement plans, businesses, etc.) and their current values?

- What are your "intangible" assets, such as education/skills, talents and interests, personal relationships, and character traits?

- What liabilities (tangible and intangible) do you need to address?

- Which of your assets or investments do you anticipate will provide you with the greatest rate of return? (Keep in mind that it helps to have clarity around your values before answering this question.)

CHAPTER 12

THE JOY OF SPENDING

The odds of going to the store for a loaf of bread and coming out with only a loaf of bread are three billion to one.

—ERMA BOMBECK

It has never been easier to part with our money. We no longer need to take a $100 bill out of our wallet or even write a check to make a purchase. We simply swipe a card, push a button, or scan our phone. Rather than driving to a store and browsing through a limited amount of physical merchandise to find something worth our time, effort, and money, we can simply go online and make a few clicks to purchase virtually anything we want. With all the convenience and estrangement from our cash, have we lost the true joy of spending? Has our financial integrity vanished in the abyss of materialistic impropriety? We are in uncharted territory, but we can use new research, as well as tried-and-true tools and techniques, to understand ourselves better—moving us in the right direction.[19] We can reconnect with the joy of spending when we make intentional choices that align with our core values, discerning between "soul needs" and "ego wants."

THE BRAIN CHEMISTRY OF SPENDING

The field of neuroeconomics (the study of economics, neuroscience, and psychology in making financial decisions) is giving us fascinating new insights into the relationship between our brains and our financial choices. We know that dopamine is a neurotransmitter that lights up and bursts like fireworks, sending sprays of energy throughout the parts of our brain that turn motivations into decisions and decisions into actions. It is the pleasure drug that floods our brains with a lovely feeling when we *think* about getting something we want. Researchers have made three profound discoveries about dopamine, with implications in our financial lives. First, actually getting what you want does *not* produce dopamine. After we make a purchase, we may feel let down, or the pleasant feeling may be fleeting. Second, the dopamine system is more interested in novel stimuli than something familiar. The marketing people know this inside and out. We are bombarded constantly and told we *need* the latest, greatest, fastest, and fanciest! Last, if the reward you expected fails to materialize, dopamine dries up, and you may experience symptoms of withdrawal. The sobering revelation in this is that we can easily become

---

19   Michalis Haliassos and Phil Thornton, "Helping People Make Good Financial Decisions: The Think Forward Initiative," VoxEU.org, April 15, 2016, http://voxeu. org/article/improving-financial-decision-making-think-forward-initiative.

consumption junkies. We become "addicted" to the chemicals being released when we expose ourselves to the daily onslaught of purchasing and spending prospects, and unless deliberately reigned in, we can succumb to self-gratification and financial mayhem.

In 2016, the average household consumer debt was about $16,000, increasing at about 11 percent per year.[20] It has become "normal" to carry consumer debt. This burden takes its toll on relational, physical, spiritual, and financial health and robs us of essential joy in life. We can take thoughtful steps to keep our brain chemistry in line for safe decision making, telling our money where to go instead of asking where it went. These three steps will help you find the joy of spending.

TELL YOUR MONEY WHERE TO GO

First, define what true prosperity means to you. Dr. Arthur Brooks of the American Enterprise Institute speaks to this in his work on happiness. We are remiss to think that more is better and that the attainment of sensory desires produces meaning and happiness in our lives. It is possible to have a thriving, growing economy that is based on fulfilling our "needs" and prioritizing our "wants." We no longer need to ride the roller-coaster economy, based on fear and greed that more often than not has our stomachs in our mouths.

Next, clarify and define your vision of what you want to create for yourself, your children, and the world. Do you desire freedom, security, health, deeper relationships, community? How do you create

---

20 Erin El Issa, "2016 American Household Credit Card Study," Nerd-Wallet, accessed June 2, 2017, https://www.nerdwallet.com/blog/average-credit-card-debt-household/.

this for today and make it viable over time? Each of your spending choices should be in accord with these key values.

Finally, create a **spending plan**. *Budget* is a bad word. It focuses on the idea of lack and deprivation. It robs everyone of personal assessment and command. "We can't spend money on that; we can't afford it." But if we create a spending plan instead, we're telling ourselves and others that we have a strategy for our financial lives, something we control and will keep us headed where we want to go as long as the plan is followed. "We are choosing not to spend money on toys because we are saving for our summer family vacation." It's all about creating the safe financial boundaries within which you can have a joyful experience. That's a spending plan. Establish what safe spending boundaries look like, and then tell your money where you want it to go.

You will find pleasure in your spending choices when you under-stand that money is a means to an end, not an end in itself. You will delight when your spending choices reflect what is important to you, feeding your soul, not just filling a perceived void, a temporary itch, or an ego desire. You will find joy by embracing contentment and in spending within safe boundaries, no matter how big or small your terrain may be!

WHAT ARE YOUR SPENDING INTENTIONS?

From the time our feet hit the floor in the morning, soap up in the shower, get dressed, and eat breakfast, we are making financial choices. We have the freedom to choose how money comes into our lives, how to give it away, how to invest it, and how we spend it on ourselves and others. Spending decisions range from the mundane to the complex, but they are increasingly becoming rote.

Choices range from our mind-sets around what we buy and why, to the tools we use to execute the monetary exchange for those purchases. It is essential that we take an arduous look at our selections and their corollaries within our families and our corporate social structures. We can have a healthy economy, environment, and personal net worth statements. It takes cognizant, creative, collaborative new ways of looking at money. Our expenditures are a good place to start.

2

Are you cheap, frugal, grandiose, or intentional?

Would you consider yourself **cheap**, **frugal**, **grandiose**, or **intentional** when it comes to making purchases? To expound, *cheap* is making a decision to buy low-price, low-quality items. *Frugal* is avoiding waste and involving little expense. *Grandiose* is an ego purchase or buying a label for its own sake. *Intentional* spending is purchasing quality, reflecting personal values, and items that will endure over time. Ponder the environmental consequences of purchasing cheap trinkets to be thrown away after one use. Contemplate ongoing purchases of high-cost, name-brand items that don't fit within your spending plan.

It seems innocuous for a family to buy and use wrapping paper. But when you hear that Americans spend more than $2.5 billion on wrapping paper, consuming tens of millions of trees and generating millions of tons of trash, the collective impact is a bit more compelling. Change starts at home, no matter how large or small.

Do you use cash or credit? The field of behavioral economics has established that we unconsciously spend more when we use credit than when we use cash.[21] The emotional centers in our brain associated with pain do not fire the same way when we use plastic, scan our phones, or push the computer button to make a purchase. When we use cash, our brains feel a bit of pain when we part with a $50 bill and get $7.48 back in change. We have become immune to the downside of our purchasing experiences, and "affluenza" (more stuff brings happiness) is running rampant. We have increasingly become disconnected with our financial choices, hence potential monetary havoc and ensuing emotional, relational, spiritual, and physical consequences bear down. Using tools and technology isn't bad; we just need to use it wisely within safe boundaries.

We decide whether to use money for our own needs and wants or to assist others in realizing theirs. Every choice has a price—not only a financial price but an opportunity cost as well. There are environmental and human costs to our financial decisions, and because of technology, we are rapidly losing touch with the connection to our financial choices.

Creating an awareness of the opportunity lost, or gained, because of your spending decision will change the way you see every choice and help you spend more effectively and efficiently.

CREATE A SPENDING PLAN

Do you remember the last time you left an all-you-can-eat buffet? Did you pile on a bit too much and leave feeling a bit too full? "I'm hungry . . . there is so much to choose from, and it all looks so good!" Maybe just a little of this and a little of that, and the next thing you

---

21   Drazen Prelac and Duncan Simester, "Always Leave Home Without It: A Further Investigation of the Credit-Card Effect on Willingness to Pay," *Marketing Letters* 12, no. 1 (2001): 5-12.

know, you are miserable. The same thing can happen in our financial lives.

Eating at an endless food buffet every day is not healthy for anyone. We also know that moderation and healthy choices bring about physical, mental, emotional, and spiritual benefits. Financial choices have the same results. Financial gluttony manifests itself in consumer debt, relational strife, and physical stress. This fiscal angst can be avoided with some planning and discipline.

A spending plan allows you to be in charge of your financial choices and their effects in the same way a diet informs your decisions about what you should and shouldn't eat to lose weight and get healthy. A spending plan provides a reference framework for the choices you make and provides you with feedback to make course corrections. Empower your family, clarify your values, and align your spending with what is important to you. A spending plan helps guide you toward accomplishing your goals and facilitates open and positive conversations by providing the safety of specific, agreed-upon boundaries that connect you and your family to a larger mission.

Develop a system that works for you—one that you will stick with and use. Research what will be the most comfortable for you. It may be a very tangible system such as using envelopes, a notepad, and pencil. For instance, let's say you have designated a certain amount of money for a month's worth of groceries. Simply put the cash in an envelope, and when the envelope is empty, you eat out of the pantry. This may sound very old-fashioned, but you reconnect with your money and you start thinking about your decisions again!

There are also websites and mobile apps such as Mint.com or Mvelopes.com that do a great job of helping you track your spending habits, or you can check with your local bank or credit union to see what they have available that integrates with your checking account. Most of these provide the capacity for managing credit cards, bank accounts, mortgages, and investments all from one hub. You can have immediate access and feedback to your financial decisions, but it does take time and discipline to set up, track, and manage.

So get to it! The sooner you put your spending plan in motion, the sooner you will see your wealth growing. Involve your family or a friend or two as well. Talk about the challenges and opportunities of doing things a bit differently today for the betterment of your tomorrow.

You are on a journey of financial maturity. It is important to understand where you are and where you want to go. You will find increasing satisfaction and fulfillment by recognizing and acknowledging who you are as a spender and deciding what small steps you want to take to lead you in a positive direction.

No matter what personal life season you are in, take time to reflect on why you are making the choices, the consequences thereof, and possible alternatives you have. Let gratefulness, your values, and thoughtful intentionality be your guide and you can't go wrong.

SHARPEN YOUR TOOLS

The concept of a spending plan is based on the notion that you are spending with intention and deliberation, with your choices reflecting what you really value and want in your life rather than conceding to a momentary feeling. Answer the following questions to help you get started devising your own spending plan.

- 🖊 What does your checkbook say about what you value?

- 🖊 What is your thought process when you make a purchase?

✐ How do you weigh your purchasing options? Is it a "soul need" or "ego want"?

✐ Do you consider the opportunity cost (the value of the best alternative forgone)?

✐ How do you feel about the purchase now, versus how will you feel about it in six months?

CHAPTER 13

"RE-WIRE, RE-FIRE"— RETIRE NO MORE!

Retirement is the ugliest word in the language.

—ERNEST HEMINGWAY

As we discussed briefly in chapter 7, financial life planning is the terminology used to describe the process of digging down deep with clients. It combines the two basic forms of understanding and analysis: the qualitative and the quantitative. The qualitative element integrates our hopes, dreams, mind-sets, values, and fears, while the quantitative element appreciates the financial tools we have in order to build a life of intention.

George Kinder, CFP, one of the fathers of this process, shares that "each of us carries within a secret yearning—a yearning that, as time and life march on, often becomes a secret sorrow. That yearning will be different for each of us, as it is the most deeply longed for expression of self. Only to the degree that we, each of us, are able to bring forth our own heart's core will our lives feel fulfilled, truly worthwhile."

Your financial journey entails so much more than just reaching a financial destination. The ideal journey is knowing you are on the right path and enjoying the ride through every life and financial season along the way. Key to any ideal journey is personal growth and embracing change. The more willing we are to explore our world and learn about what we discover, the richer our journey will be.

NEW ENDEAVORS

It is a journey that may find us leaving a career, but let's not "retire." To retire is defined as "to withdraw from, remove oneself, or to fall back in retreat." This life season definition is as defunct as clipping bond coupons for income! Mitch Anthony, in his book *The New Retirementality*, challenges us, "We need a sexier term for retirement. It doesn't fit anymore." Maybe they aren't exactly sexy, but I like "rewirement" or "refirement," both of which imbue the idea of involvement, engagement, and entering into something exciting. It is no longer a question of what we are retiring from but what we are *rewiring* to and why.

Demographic, societal, technological, and workplace trends have converged to offer a new winter season of life and finance that is much more fluid and flexible than the one our parents experienced or that we have been allowed to dream of until recently. We are debunking the myth that governmental agencies and financial services institutions have fed us that retirement is a one-time event that will allow us to disengage from the rat race and immerse ourselves in a life of ease. While initially that sounds enticing, research is finding that staying active and engaged in some type of work that offers a sense of purpose will help each of us to live longer and healthier in all aspects of our lives.

Today, I have clients who intentionally embark on new endeavors that bring meaning and fulfillment to their lives alongside their leisure pursuits. My husband, Mark, is on the cusp of his second "rewirement." In 2007 he shifted gears into a fulfilling season of high school academia. He is now looking forward to pursuing his passions in new ways to permeate his days. A competent, honorable, life financial advisor will help you balance vacation with vocation and make sure your financial pieces are in place to provide you with the means to make it happen.

While it doesn't prevent aging, Dr. John Rowe and Dr. Robert Kahn have documented more than ten years of research to show that the three main components of successful aging include: avoiding disease, maintaining high cognitive and physical function, and actively engaging in life. And in her book *I Could Do Anything, If I Only Knew What It Was*, author Barbara Sher writes, "You'll never be happy just amusing yourself. . . . Even in retirement, when you are looking to get off the fast track and 'smell the roses,' you should be pushing past what you merely enjoy into what has real meaning to you." Yes, leisure in all seasons of life is important to maintaining good health, but too much free time as you move into your personal fall can lead to indifference, complacency, and lethargy.

Remember, good physical, relational, spiritual, financial, and intellectual health is not a benefit bestowed on a lucky few in a single season. They are the harvest of day-to-day choices, cultivated with education, discipline, discernment, and an abundant sprinkling of blessings throughout all seasons.

We need to recognize and assimilate the fact that our financial fields to harvest are changing. Two of the three traditional fields—pensions and Social Security—do not have the same impact and capacity they had in years past. We need to take personal responsibility to cultivate two other fields—our personal asset fields and the opportunities found in the new "sharing economy." We can both minimize expenses and create new income streams from the technology, creativity, and community collaboration options at our fingertips. Let's take a look at what is changing as we seek to optimally harvest from the array of fields available to us.

FOUR FIELDS TO HARVEST: PENSIONS, SOCIAL SECURITY, PERSONAL SAVINGS, AND THE SHARING ECONOMY

Pensions—In days of old, there were huge fields of pension plans that employees would harvest upon their retirement. Pension plans helped with employee recruitment and retention and provided predictable income for employees moving into retirement. These defined benefit pension plans are quickly becoming a crop of the past. As we now know, no longer do people work for a company for thirty-plus years and retire, receiving a gold watch and a financial payout that will last the rest of their lives. Companies have experienced increased funding volatility with demographic and economic cycle fluctuations, and the Pension Protection Act of 2006 made the rules more complex for participation. The result was such that companies are now finding it more cost efficient and effective to shift the responsibility of preparing for future income into the hands of the employees.

Social Security—Not to be taken lightly, this financial field needs to be harvested carefully. There are over five hundred different withdrawal strategies, and the difference between a good one and a bad one can amount to hundreds of thousands of dollars. Once you start taking withdrawals, there is little room to revisit. You only have twelve months to change your mind after you start taking your benefit, and you would need to repay everything that you had received for yourself or any family members.

If you claim too early, you lock in payments that are reduced for each month you claim. If you take your payments too late, you may experience a lower quality of life and possibly leave money on the table if you die in your late sixties or early seventies.

Determining when and how to apply for Social Security benefits is very personal and is weighted by many factors, including life expectancy, marital status, whether you are continuing to work, other assets available for cash flow, income needed, and other economic or personal situations.

Bottom line, Social Security is a harvest that keeps producing. You can't outlive its income stream, but you can make mistakes in your thinking and your decision making before taking it. This makes it vitally important to maximize what you will be able to receive and strategize how it is going to work alongside your other income sources.

Personal Savings—If properly cultivated over the years, this should be your largest and most prolific field from which to harvest. Personal assets may include personal retirement plans like IRAs and Roths; employer-sponsored retirement plans such as a 401(k), SEP, SIMPLE, or 403(b); business interests; nonqualified investments; stock options; annuities; cash value life insurances; home equity; and hard assets such as precious metals and real estate.

As you tap into your financial storehouses and start to utilize and enjoy the fruits of your labor, be prudent and discerning. Tax laws change, and depending on our political flavor of the moment, they will have a large impact on your distribution phase (fall) as you move on to preparing for the legacy phase (winter). How much do you need? You will normally spend more in the "go-go years" shortly following your shift away from full-time work. There is an emotional and mental shift when you no longer have the nine-to-five routine, and the financial implications need to be embraced. Many people underestimate what they will spend during this first phase of "rewirement." Inflation, health care costs, taxes on the sale of assets, income from a variety of sources, inheritance decisions, and shifts in the economic environment all need to be considered as you create a sustainable distribution plan. Your harvest needs to provide for the go-go years, the slow-go years, and the no-go years.

Your harvest needs to provide for the go-go years, the slow-go years, and the no-go years.

In 1994 financial planner William Bengen researched a variety of withdrawal rates on a retirement portfolio (all assets lumped together). Using historical returns, he found that 4 percent was the highest rate that was sustainable over a thirty-year period. That has been the status quo for the past twenty-three years. This might have worked in a long-standing bull market, but economic and personal life seasons have changed, and investors need to reconsider their tactics. The old wisdom did not consider the higher spending desired in the go-go years or the increasing costs of health care in the "no-go" years.

How do you create sustainability for the life expectancy and variables you will encounter? It is imperative to understand how taking money out of different "buckets" will affect your taxes in ever-changing tax environments. You want to coordinate the best way to tap Social Security, pensions, personal retirement accounts, annuities, and other income resources. What is the current economic environment? Are you exposed to interest rate risk or sequence of return risk (the risk of maintaining distributions in down markets)?

The market has moved into a rising interest rate season, raising the risk in bond prices. We continue to see market volatility and have seen market expansion since March 2009, boding well for past distributions. What if the market incurs a major pullback, triggering a recession? It isn't a matter of *if* but *when*. Consider the impact on your portfolio of taking money out in a down market—this is managing sequence of return risk. Have you considered what you want to leave for family or causes close to your heart? Creating a strategy based on the complexity of your financial resources will optimize how you use your resources today and create the legacy for tomorrow.

Many people believe the myth that they don't need to do any planning in their personal life harvest season because they already did that it in the summer "accumulation" phase. They set their goals, diversified, and rebalanced. They have resources in "buckets." They attained a "number." They did a lot of things right! They think that now that the distribution phase is upon them, they can sit back and relax.

The truth is that when you combine the intricacies and nuances of your financial resources with the emotional, psychological, spiritual, relational and physical changes that lie ahead of you, there is still a lot of planning to do. You can spend your life in reactionary mode or take the proactive approach, embrace change, and find the right team to walk alongside you to accomplish what is important. Do your homework, then set to task. It is not about a product but a process. It is about making course corrections along the way, knowing that life is full of bumps and there is no perfect recipe for success. It is about being intentional, thoughtful, and joyful along the way. It is about living in your full potential, utilizing your true wealth.

With the right financial advocates and guides to help you steer on an increasingly complex journey, you will have a better opportunity to savor the moment and decrease the likelihood of future regret. You will trek through the "go-go" years and the "slow-go" years and then settle into the "no-go" years. There are financial decisions and implications that need to be defined and refined along the way.

The New Sharing Economy—The Internet is changing the way we bring money into our lives. We can avail ourselves of new avenues that still incorporate integrity, dignity, competency, grace, and joy. As we look at utilizing and leveraging these resources, we can incorporate their innovative, creative aspects into all our life seasons. The sharing economy and collaborative consumption is changing the way we do our accumulation and distribution years, with opportunities never before experienced.

There are three major drivers in this new environment. **Customer behavior** is changing. People are becoming open and flexible to new ideas around using what they have to benefit themselves and others. **Online social networking and electronic markets** make it easy to transfer money or check out personal profiles to build trust. **Mobile devices** make shared goods and services more convenient than ever before. While on the road, people can find a place to stay while their spouse is driving them to the next destination or book someone to stay at their home!

No longer needed is the second home in warmer weather that can become a financial, emotional, and time liability. We can use websites such as SeniorHomeExchange.com, HolidayExchange.com, Airbnb.com, or HomeExchange.com to look at ways to utilize our primary residences and minimize expenses for traveling to locales on our bucket list.

Websites and apps such as Taskrabbit, Uber, Airbnb, and Dogvacay are enabling people to earn money on their own time frame using human and capital assets already at hand. This opens up doors for creating work–life balance. We can get paid for something we enjoy doing or have had as a hobby for years.

While change is hard, and many details are unclear as to how the "gig economy" plays out with taxation and licensing issues, the benefits of the sharing economy are numerous. It will build stronger families and communities as we share experiences and embrace that we have more similarities than differences. It reduces the environmental impact of everyone having their own (vacation home, boat, bicycle, lawnmower, etc.) The cost savings or income opportunities will impact and increase the prospect for longevity of our financial buckets.

It is worth exploring if and how the sharing economy fits into your financial and life harvest seasons. Our family has traded our home in order to make travel more affordable when our four kids were young, and we have shared our home and our community on Airbnb, HomeExchange, and CouchSurfing. We have had nothing but delightful experiences and engaging encounters.

How is your gratitude journal looking?

SHARPEN YOUR TOOLS

As you embrace what a financial harvest will look like in your fall life season, consider:

- 🖋 Instead of retiring from—what are you rewiring for?

- 🖋 What emotional considerations do you need to make for this life transition?

- 🖋 How will your income streams shift and what do you need to do to optimize them?

- 🖋 Is there a facet of the "sharing economy" that you would like to explore and cultivate?

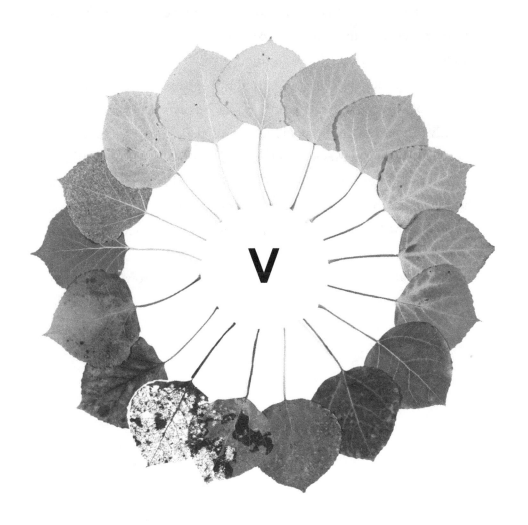

WINTER: LOSS AND LEGACY

Winter is a season of dualities. It is a time when past and future, life and death, challenge and opportunity all coalesce to keep the life cycle in motion. As a life season, winter can be a deeply painful time—one in which death, illness, divorce, and disasters are experienced. Financial winters can include all the financial ramifications of a life winter, seen in economic recessions or depressions, unemployment, bankruptcies, and foreclosures.

By preparing for or learning from this season of loss, you will be able to bloom anew in the spring. It is a deeply spiritual and introspective time. For those in the winter of their lives, decisions and directives in how to preserve their hopes, dreams, lessons, and values, as well as how to best pass down their financial assets, will create a lasting legacy. For those who have experienced a financial winter, it is an opportunity to glean great wisdom and to bloom anew. Economic winters also provide a unique opportunity to invest when prices are down or start a new company as new needs arise, to sow the seeds to thrive in the seasons to come.

CHAPTER 14

PREPARING FOR WINTER

Winter is on my head, but eternal spring is in my heart.

—VICTOR HUGO

Like their climatic namesakes, the transition from an economic fall to an economic winter can happen very quickly. We may see telltale clouds on the horizon, but many times, markets can spiral down into a recession, or a depression, with little warning. With world economies in flux, political personalities and policies at play, and technology at our fingertips, markets experience more volatility than ever before. Closer to home, companies may be forced to issue a hiring freeze, cut overtime, or even resort to layoffs. When these types of financial blizzards come (and they will), individuals, families, and companies will need to tap into their reserves, tighten their belts, reassess their priorities, and hunker down until the blue skies and sunshine of spring make their triumphant return.

Winter can certainly be a brutal financial season, but if you have prepared properly, economic winters can be the ideal time to take advantage of the growth cycle to follow. Investors often use an economic winter to "get in" and capitalize on the deep discounts offered when prices are down, whether they be on homes, businesses for sale, or stock shares.

Warren Buffett says that we should "be fearful when others are greedy and be greedy when others are fearful." The late, great global investor John Templeton said, "The time of maximum pessimism is the best time to buy and the time of maximum optimism is the best time to sell." When there is irrational exuberance in any of the markets, know that it is time to harvest; there is an economic winter around the corner.

We can't alter or change our natural seasons, and from our personal perspective, we can't always control or easily predict our economic seasons either. We can, however, anticipate, prepare, and reap the most out of the opportunities inherent in each. With proper preparation, we can at least minimize the impact and temper the fear of each winter economic season.

One of the best ways to prepare for a winter financial season is to have the proper tools in place. Do you have a solid savings account? Whether it be in your business or personal life, you need to have something set aside to fall back on. The amount you should have can vary a bit depending on your life season and other financial resources available to you. For example, if you are in your fall life season and are collecting over 50 percent of your needs from Social Security and a pension, I usually suggest that you have a year or two of supplemental expenses set aside in liquid savings. This would help you to minimize the impact of a market correction on your investment account and curtail your sequence of return risk. If you have a solid savings account, you have the opportunity to sow it into opportunities that present themselves in winter. Buy when prices are down! This simple but very powerful tool will help you shovel out of a financial or economic winter.

Another powerful way to prepare for a winter is to know how your financial tools can work for you and what your options are before you need to react. Do you have cash value in a life insurance policy? Should you consider taking a loan off of it, doing a partial surrender, or cashing it out in the event of a financial hardship? Do you have a 401(k) at work? Does it have loan provisions? Do you have equity in your home that you could access? Would it be better to refinance or take out a home equity line of credit? Don't wait until there is five feet of snow in your driveway before you get a snow blower or hope yours has gas in it or try to get it to work efficiently. Make sure you know what tools you have and how they work in the event of an emergency.

SHARPEN YOUR TOOLS

Being prepared for lean times will allow you to move through them more productively.

- 🌿 Do you have a solid savings account built up? If not, when do you want to start paying yourself first?

- 🌿 What financial tools do you have, and do you know how they are working for you?

- 🌿 Who will be affected by your proper preparation for a financial winter?

- 🌿 What benefits or opportunities would you like to pursue in a financial winter?

CHAPTER 15

PASSING ON THE ASSETS THAT REALLY COUNT

A rich person should leave his kids enough to do anything but not enough to do nothing.

—WARREN BUFFETT

Every three years I get together with over three hundred of my closest relatives for a family reunion. Okay, most of them are cousins twice removed, and as the years go by, I know fewer of them, but we are related. We spend three days visiting, playing family trivia, bidding on memorabilia, dancing, eating, and drinking. We remember those who have gone before us and share dreams of what lies ahead. Normally innocuous, a recent gathering landed one of my cousins in jail for assault. It seems a fistfight broke out and she drew blood with a punch thrown at her sister.

The talk back at the hotel was very matter of fact: the fight was over money. It felt a bit like one of comedian Jeff Foxworthy's monologues: "If your family does their estate planning over a beer and a fistfight, you might be a redneck!" I wanted to laugh, but it also broke my heart. Long-simmering emotions erupted over how my still-living uncle was dividing up land and not communicating well with his eleven children.

A bit of drama added some excitement to the weekend, but how sad that greed and resentment over money caused potential long-term damage. I have worked with enough clients to know that this incident in our family isn't an isolated one; it is a systemic illness that can infect and destroy anyone's family.

At the very start of your estate planning, you need to ask yourself several questions. The first is perhaps the most important: For what do you want to be remembered? Chances are it isn't solely about the family checkbook. More people focus on financial estate planning than they do passing on the assets that really count. If you want a sustainable financial legacy, you need to prioritize giving other endowments first. Your family values, beliefs, and history will create greater wealth than any stock portfolio or business empire ever will. It will also create the strong foundation to battle the "shirtsleeve-to-shirtsleeve" adage, which assumes that first-generation wealth is likely to be lost by the third generation.

You should also qualify and quantify your financial assets in order to incorporate what you can control and then position them appropriately. Likewise, you have to embrace, and be at peace with, that which you cannot control.

Deciding how much money you will need or want in your "rewirement" years is the kick off to discerning how much is appropriate for your heirs. Take the time for some deep processing to get clarity on these decisions, as they are about so much more than just money. This won't always be easy, of course. For most, what we inherit is symbolic of our relationship with our predecessor, making clear and honest communication an even more important practice than usual around these particular financial decisions.

As evident in my own family's story, emotions can quickly boil over when deciding what is transferred and to whom, no matter the amount of wealth or types of assets involved. My family moved quickly to resolve my cousins' literal fistfight. We gathered the following Sunday morning for the traditional military recognition and balloon-release ceremony for family members who were no longer with us. My cousin's son—a pastor—gave a talk on forgiveness and moving forward with what it means to be family. I am blessed with a rich heritage from my immigrant grandparents, a deep commitment to family and work ethic based on integrity and fortitude. I am committed to handling my family financial affairs without bloodshed. I am also committed to helping you do the same.

PREPARING THE FIELDS: THE PERILS, PROCESSES, AND PURPOSES OF TRANSFERRING WEALTH

When you think of estate planning, what comes to mind? Discussions or documents? Attitudes or attorneys? Discernment or death? Conversations or control? Timely transitions or tax efficiencies?

Your answers reveal something more than just your personal preferences or perceptions. They form the biggest differences between the governing principles of the **wealth transfer** process and the practical realities of **traditional estate planning**. Both are needed, but wisdom in process and application is essential to either experience. If you are going to transfer financial wealth, make sure you pass on insight and sound judgment *first*. Wealth rarely creates wisdom! You would not let someone fly a plane who is not competent at the controls, and it's the same with wealth. Money is a complex tool that, as your life becomes more complicated, needs to be passed on prudently and proficiently to those competent enough to receive it.

I can't emphasize enough that communication is paramount to any successful estate planning experience. It is okay to talk about money with your children, and you should do so often as you make decisions not just in estate planning but throughout every life and financial season with them. Behind every financial decision, there is a teachable moment. It's our job as parents to pass as much of that knowledge on to our children as we can. You wouldn't hand a loaded gun to an adult child without proper training, nor would you do so without having a good sense of their mental and emotional state of being. Leaving financial assets can cause great harm, if not used properly, to ill-edified heirs. It is dangerous and irresponsible to both your heirs and those who may be affected by their decisions. As a benefactor, it is your responsibility to ensure that the terms, conditions, intentions, and expectations associated with your assets are thoroughly communicated to your beneficiaries. If not you, after all, then who will?

Bring in professionals to assist you, but make the time to do it properly. You can creatively leverage what you leave by using charitable remainder trusts and a family of other tools that minimize what goes to the government and maximizes what goes to those you care about. Look at it this way: Don't you want to do your giving while you're living, so you know where it's going?

Don't you want to do your giving while you're living, so you know where it's going?

The traditional estate planning process primarily revolves around documents and should be done as your financial situation changes over time, usually every five to ten years. You must prepare for the fact that the wealth transfer process involves ongoing conversations with family members as the context of your life changes and asking yourself questions like:

- How old are you and how old are your children or heirs?

- Is there unity in the family?

- What family dynamics or considerations are you aware of?

- What is the nature of your wealth (inherited, created)?

Remember, considerations like these are much more dynamic than just the surface transition of material assets.

Ron Blue says, "If you love your children equally, you will treat them *uniquely*." You need to understand what the ramifications of your decisions may or may not be for each of your heirs. Also, keep in mind that even children raised in the same family will handle money differently, so you want to take the time to discuss what is best for each of your children or heirs. Never manipulate behavior, and never let money matters come between spouses or between parent and child either. By doing so, you may deny them the opportunity to find fulfillment through meaningful employment or their need to provide for their own family.

Understand that your family has a set of unique character assets and liabilities that run much deeper than what sits on the surface of the financial balance sheet. You would be wise to find out what those personality assets and liabilities are and, more importantly, what value or risk they bring to your family.

You may want to help your family bloom with their intellectual capital by giving them money to further their education or life skills. Perhaps you're considering investing in their human capital. Does a child or your spouse want to start or build a business? If so, what do their character assets and liabilities look like? How can their interests, skills, talents, and work or life experience be leveraged in a business endeavor?

While considerably more difficult to discuss, a family's liabilities must be addressed as well. Liabilities can take many forms, but most simply defined, they are anything that may threaten the personal or financial well-being of you and your heirs after the wealth transfer is complete. A family member with special needs who may not be able to financially support themselves, a familial estrangement, or a financial asset with the potential to depreciate or incur costs—such as a vehicle, home, business, stock portfolio, or other investment—all constitute a liability.

Calculating your family's liabilities is admittedly stressful, and the conversations they require are often uncomfortable. As a result, it's easy to overlook liabilities, and it's even easier to avoid discussing the ones we do see. Failing to prepare for the liabilities of a wealth transfer only jeopardizes your efforts, however, by endangering the well-being of those you care about and leaving them with the burdens of finding solutions to problems they may or may not have known existed. Whatever they are, you will need to identify your liabilities and determine the best plan for minimizing or eliminating the risks they present.

These types of questions need to be discussed in detail with your loved ones as your life circumstances change. That means the most important piece in the wealth transfer process will be "The Talk." Whether you convene a family conference or approach each of your heirs individually, communicating your reasoning behind your transfer decisions is the best defense against the harm caused by uncertainty later. How you present your expectations, and the details of the process, will depend on your unique set of financial circumstances and family dynamics. Starting the discussions and discerning direction before any decisions are irreversible will ensure a smoother transfer and a much better experience for everyone involved. Ideally, you want your wealth transfer process to be *timely*, *purposeful*, and *meaningful*.

Ideally, you want your wealth transfer process to be *timely*, *purposeful*, and *meaningful*.

On Christmas day one year, for example, I opened a small box from my aunt. Accustomed to the traditional gift of brandy-laced fruitcake, I was taken aback as her wedding ring peered back brightly out of the box. "I wanted you to have it now," she said, "so I could watch you enjoy it." That she did! She would proclaim to her tablemates at assisted living, "That is my ring. Isn't it pretty on her?" Even as she slipped into dementia, I would hold her hand and she would touch it—reconnecting with fond, unspoken memories. Family relationships and the personal well-being that comes from good ones are much more valuable than money. They are the priceless assets that can offer our lives true joy and meaning.

Current 2017 estate tax laws allow you to give up to $14,000 to anyone and everyone you want without having to file a gift tax return. The current lifetime exclusion that you can give away without incurring gift or estate taxes is $5,450,000. You don't need to die to pass this on, which is why the timing component in wealth transfer is very important. Once you set your personal financial finish lines and decide how much is enough for yourself, you can decide if it is appropriate and wise to pass financial resources on to your heirs sooner than later. If you want to give while you are alive, make sure there are no strings attached and that you are giving with purpose. You want to give in ways that will truly help your heirs help themselves, not hinder them from their potential.

The fear of making the wrong decisions for your heirs and the inherent uncertainties of a wealth transfer have led many people to want to "control from the grave." Financial institutions are creating complex products to address this desire. But the truth is, you can't truly control anything once you are gone, and you really won't care. Doesn't it make more sense to properly prepare those who will be affected by your financial legacy while you are living, passing on your values, insights, dreams, and desires in a way that can be fulfilled and lived out after you are gone? It's that idea that forms the basis for creating an **ethical will**. An ethical will is a beautiful component of a healthy wealth transfer, serving as a proclamation of your personal values, your spiritual beliefs, and your hopes and dreams for future generations. It can also contain elements of forgiveness and emanate grace.

Traditional estate planning comprises the legal elements of wealth transfer, making its role in the process integral to its success. Traditional estate planning uses five primary legal tools to negotiate the transfer of wealth: **will and testaments, trusts, powers of attorney, medical directives,** and **living wills**. Depending on the complexity of your financial life, you will want to have one or more professionals walking alongside you as you prepare to implement any of these options. A good estate planning professional will guide you through the inner workings of each of these tools, and others, to determine which are best for your needs and how to properly utilize them.

Choose your team wisely when planning your estate. Make sure that whomever you hire understands what you are trying to accomplish and is willing to walk you through the process, not just produce paperwork. Your team may include a Certified Financial Planner, attorney, tax professional, trust officer, insurance professional, and planned giving specialist, but make sure all of these professionals are willing to work together for your benefit.

As you gather all of your financial details and personally reflect on what you hope to accomplish in your estate planning and wealth transfer process, communicate, communicate, communicate! Whether with family members or financial professionals, make sure everything is out on the table—complexities are embraced, intentions are clearly understood, and options are fully addressed.

Take Rick, for example. He was a serial entrepreneur with a number of businesses. Some of his children were involved and wanted to be a part of the succession plan, while others did not. One child wanted to be a part of the family business but had some personal problems that needed to be addressed first. Should the parents divide everything up equally?

This is often a recipe for disaster. Explore the family dynamics a little more closely, and there's often a better strategy and set of tools that would best serve each individual member of the family and the family as a whole.

To apply this strategy to your own situation, you will first need to have a firm understanding of the complexities of personalities and assets that exist within your family. Gather as much information as you can on the many assets and liabilities of your family before deciding what should be done with them. Wise decisions cannot be made in the absence of knowledge.

As you move through the wealth transfer process, having had meaningful conversations with your heirs and advisors, tools such as trusts or wills serve as legally binding contracts solidifying your decisions. The advantage of having the right tools in place is to make sure you get to choose who will receive your assets when you pass away, as well as dictate who will take charge over your minor children. For instance, maybe you want to have different people serve as your children's guardians from those who will be a trustee of your financial positions. A will is your only opportunity to turn what would otherwise be a preference or request into a legally binding directive. If you do not have a will, the courts will appoint a guardian of minor children for you, along with all other decisions on how to distribute your estate.

Probating a will is a court process that supervises the transfer of assets, a process that can take about a year to work through. You can minimize or avoid probate in several ways, but how you title assets will help most of all. A discussion with professional advisors is best for this approach. Without a deep understanding of the legal complexities associated with structuring assets and filing the necessary paperwork, you are more likely to submit mistakes that may be expensive, time-consuming, or even impossible to reverse. By simply titling your assets as "Transfer on Death," for instance, they will be legally obligated to go directly to a beneficiary rather than through the terms of your will or trust. Any type of contractual agreement with beneficiary designations, such as life insurance, annuities, and retirement plans, will also go directly to beneficiaries and avoid the probate process. It is important to review your primary and contingent beneficiary designations occasionally. Your life circumstances will change as you move through life seasons.

Medical health care directives are another critical component of estate planning. The health landscape is changing rapidly, so knowing that your voice will be heard through a legal document when it may not be physically possible to speak can be a great relief to family members or friends. The living will and durable power of attorney for health care are governed by individual states, so you will need to check with resident attorneys in your state(s) of residency for specifics.

Again, communication during the transfer of wealth is paramount and must be maintained throughout the process. Make sure that you talk about these very personal decisions with family members, friends, clergy, and your personal physician. Make sure these legal documents are accessible and available and that the executor, trustee, trusted family, and friends know where they are located. That means keeping your estate planning documents in a secure place, such as a safe. You should also keep an inventory of all your assets, liabilities, account numbers, and titling information someplace where family or friends know how to access it. Many people use an online "vault" or just write out the inventory in hard copy, such that it can be reviewed and updated as warranted.

As you gain knowledge and glean wisdom around wealth transfer and estate planning, you will create peace of mind as you put the moving pieces together. You, your trustee, and your heirs should have a clear understanding of how every aspect of your financials should be divided up and cared for, ideally with a well-reasoned explanation why. Remember that by clarifying your intent and purpose, you can greatly minimize or alleviate the potential for confusion, hurt, speculation, and fighting. Above all, however, the conversations you have around your family stories, values, hopes, dreams, and expectations will provide the firm foundation for a successful transfer of your true wealth.

SHARPEN YOUR TOOLS

Successfully transferring wealth begins well before the winter season of your financial life. You should lay the groundwork by sharing financial wisdom and knowledge with your potential heirs and communicating your values to them on a regular basis throughout every life season. During the winter season, though, these conversations become even more important. To help build a framework for these discussions, start by answering the following questions.

- *❧* To create your "family balance sheet," what human, intellectual, financial, and social capital or liabilities do you have?

- *❧* Are your heirs ready to constructively receive their financial inheritance?

- *❧* Do you believe it is your responsibility to prepare them?

- *❧* Have you shared your story as well as your estate planning documents with your adult children?

- *❧* What types of conversations do you have with those who will be affected by your financial choices? Are there fences you need to mend, forgiveness to seek, forgiveness to extend?

CHAPTER 16

RELATIONSHIP WINTERS

Even death is not to be feared by one who has lived wisely.

—BUDDHA

Death is inevitable and can be devastating. Whether it's a physical death or a relational death like a divorce, the timing and circumstances of these "relationship winters" are often unexpected and always profoundly painful. The emotional pain of losing a loved one will usually lessen over time, but it will always be a part of our lives.

We will all have to weather relational winters; they are a difficult, sad component of life. Along with the emotional pain incurred from a relational winter, many come with significant financial distress as well. If there's any consolation from these tragic storms, it's that we can at least anticipate our eventual encounter with them and do our best to be financially prepared.

Bringing in the appropriate professionals to assist you in your planning process is wise, as is putting your family and friend support system into place. The conversations you have are the key to reducing the devastation afterward. These conversations may be uncomfortable, but they are powerfully important in minimizing the emotional and financial damage. Perhaps even more importantly, they also offer people a chance to affirm meaningful relationships they may have otherwise taken for granted.

Part of the healing process is to embrace the grieving process. In both my professional and personal life, I've seen how differently people handle grief. Some hold their feelings in or deny that their loved one is gone until they can accept the loss, while others immediately and openly grieve. Regardless of how we do it, we all must understand how important grieving is to our well-being and to the legacy of our loved ones. The sorrow of losing a loved one takes time—months or even years—so remember to be gracious to yourself or others who are in the midst of it.

Every personal winter is unique and profound in experience and expression. Make sure you surround yourself with the support of people who will walk alongside you. Family and friends who are willing to listen and provide tangible support with childcare, cooking, errands, and needed diversions should also be cherished—and their offerings should be accepted; you need and deserve their help. Community support groups, therapists, counselors, or other professionals will provide insight and assistance. Spiritual guidance from a priest, pastor, rabbi, or other person of faith can provide much-needed comfort as well. You are not alone, and together with your entrusted community, the healing will begin.

As the pain abates, you can look at putting your financial affairs in order. That doesn't mean that you should begin buying and selling assets. Any significant financial decisions should not be made immediately after the loss of a loved one, whether by way of a physical death or a marital one. Refrain from making any substantial financial gifts or major decisions—where you are going to live, for instance—for at least a year, if possible. However, some things warrant addressing as soon as possible.

Your first move will be to *gather* all of your financial documents, such as marriage and birth certificates, life insurance policies, and your spouse's Social Security and any veterans benefit statements. Next, *contact* your insurance agent for assistance in filing the death claim, your estate attorney to assist you in the estate settlement process, your financial advisor to assist in notifying custodians, and your spouse's employer or their HR office to file for any benefits. *Obtain at least* a dozen copies of the death certificate from the funeral director. *Inquire* at the Social Security Administration about what benefits are available to you. *Pay* any bills that are currently due, and close any credit cards held solely in your spouse's name. Have a friend or family member alongside you as you do these things, as your mind will likely be blurry and it may be hard to focus.

The following steps can be done over time, but doing so at a timely pace is best. The first is to retitle assets that were held jointly, such as real estate, vehicles, and businesses. You and your spouse may have owned your home for years. Your original cost basis is your purchase price plus any improvement costs. If there has been a summer of economic growth, your home has gone up in value. If your home has appreciated and was jointly titled, then you should get a new appraisal. If you are a widow(er), you will receive a step up in cost basis for inheriting your spouse's share, which will benefit you down the road if you decide to sell the home.

In a divorce, you will be dividing a household. If you have children, your overall expenses will go up with the complexities of two households. You will need to tackle important financial questions, transitioning from married to single: What will be your new spending needs? Who will be in charge of what? Will you or your former spouse need to go back to work? How will this affect the childcare? Looking at current and future value, tax, and liquidity issues is imperative. You need to thoroughly vet all the assets available, including future pension and Social Security. Many times spouses have accumulated assets inside a 401(k) or IRA. There are tax and penalty consequences of doing this incorrectly, so it's best to ask the court to issue a qualified domestic relations order (QDRO). A QDRO will determine what portion of the assets should be moved into the other spouse's name.

Whether divorced or a widow(er), you will have to update your information at any of your credit card, insurance, or other financial institutions. This is also a good time to contact the three credit bureaus—Equifax, Experian, and TransUnion—and let them know your change in marital status. Once you have notified your financial institutions and changed the proper titles, you will have time to closely review your documents for any insurance coverage or other benefits that perhaps you didn't know about, such as with professional organizations, government agencies, or unions.

Following a death or divorce, it's wise to work with your attorney and financial advisors to determine what debts and/or taxes must be paid during this time as well. The requirements and options available to you are frustratingly complex, especially in the wake of a tragedy. A qualified and competent professional will be able to help you reduce debts and navigate your taxes. Plus, it's a good opportunity to discuss with your financial advisor the most advantageous way to take benefits, including from Social Security, pensions, and retirement accounts.

After the healing from a relational winter takes hold, at your own pace, you can begin redefining your personal goals moving forward. You will want to review your own estate plan and make sure beneficiary designations are up to date on life insurance policies, retirement accounts, and employee benefit programs. You can create a new financial plan that will give you peace of mind as you move forward and start blooming again.

SHARPEN YOUR TOOLS

Whether it's a death, divorce, or other relational winter, the impact is felt on all facets of your life. The financial ramifications can be significant, complicated, and enduring. Answering the following questions can help prepare you for any relationship winters you will face.

- 🌿 Do you have an updated will or estate plan?

- 🌿 Do you have a living will, power of medical directive, power of attorney?

- 🌿 Where do you keep important paperwork and passwords?

- 🌿 What financial tools do you have that will sustain your family if you are not present?

- 🌿 Do you need to review beneficiary designations?

CHAPTER 17

EMBRACE THE CHALLENGE OF CHANGE

Our brains are either our greatest assets or our greatest liabilities.

—ROBERT KIYOSAKI

I sat in the driver's seat and carefully looked both ways as I pulled the car out of the rental agency. I turned on the right blinker and was met with the windshield wipers furiously crossing my path. So it went. For the first several days of driving on the left side of the road in Australia, the windshield wipers worked beautifully every time I went to make a turn.

It was so hard to change something as simple as using the left-hand-side control. It was comical—I had to think about something that was rote behavior. The consequence of my ongoing faux pas was negligible, and my family just chuckled. However, the first time I forgot to look right for oncoming traffic made a much bigger impact (almost literally) to my psyche and changed my driving habits immediately.

Making changes in your financial habits may feel more complex than driving on the opposite side of the road, but consider the similarities. Both demand that you force yourself to do something that at first feels unnatural, unsafe, uncomfortable, and inconvenient. Most of us set financial resolutions at some point in our lives. Possibly to save more, make more, spend less, give more, or set goals. Maybe you dig a little deeper and decide that you want to communicate better, reconnect with your assets, or rebalance your portfolio. Many times, though, much of your resolve is stalled in the remnants of old habits that are hard to break. You're not alone.

In the 1990s, Dr. Edward Miller, a former CEO of Johns Hopkins Medicine and dean of Johns Hopkins University School of Medicine, famously announced that nine out of ten of his hospital's patients who had undergone painful, invasive, expensive bypass heart surgery refused to make the necessary lifestyle changes to avoid repeat surgery or even death. "If you look at people after coronary-artery bypass grafting two years later, 90 percent of them have not changed their lifestyle," Miller said. "And that's been studied over and over and over again. And so we're missing some link in there. Even though they know they have a very bad disease and they know they should change their lifestyle, for whatever reason, they can't."[22]

If the fear of death itself could not motivate 90 percent of these patients to alter their habits, what does this mean for the rest of us? Is it futile to think we can change any of our habits? Dr. Dean Ornish,

---

22   Alan Deutschman, "Change or Die," Fast Company website, posted May 1, 2005, https://www.fastcompany.com/52717/change-or-die.

founder of the Preventive Medicine Research Institute, didn't think so. In 1993, Dr. Ornish conducted his own study alongside Mutual of Omaha and discovered that lifestyle change *did* happen in people who took a holistic approach to transformation. Those subjects found a new vision of the "joy of living" by looking at all aspects of their lives—the psychological, emotional, and spiritual dimensions—alongside the nuts and bolts of health information. With these new motivators, the study found only 33 percent of patients didn't stick with their program.[23]

HOW TO CHANGE HABITS

To change a habit, picture what the consequences will be if you don't make a change and feel the fear. Depending on your pain tolerance, you may make a shift sooner than later! Next, create and embrace a beautiful vision of what lies on the other side of the adjustment. Make it tangible. Journal, collage, converse, and collaborate with others. Make it real to you and to the people in your life who are affected by this behavioral course correction. Find accountability partners, mentors, coaches, or advisors as needed.

What does a healthy financial life look like to you?

Who will be impacted by your decision to pursue health?

What will happen if you don't make the necessary changes?

---

23 Molly O'Neill, "Unusual Heart Therapy Wins Coverage from Large Insurer," *New York Times*, July 28, 1993.

Our innate nature wants to pull us back to what we think is "normal." This is called homeostasis or equilibrium in the world of biology, and it's the notion that our bodies are working hard to create feedback loops that help keep biological functions in a balanced routine.

We have financial routines, too. For example, you may stop at the local coffee shop every day for your favorite cup of java. You may buy food from the discount section at the grocery store. Our daily financial routines are governed by our environment, mind-sets, predispositions, and feedback methods, among others. When we try to change, we are pressing against our previous version of "normal," and our mental feedback loops are going to resist. So focus on small wins with financial change! For instance, how do you want to make a 1 percent improvement or build on a success by 1 percent? In the previous examples, does making coffee at home one day a week sound palatable? Does choosing only healthy options from the discount bin add additional value to an already good routine?

LET GO OF THE GUILT

We should save for the future. We should spend less than we bring in. We should enjoy life within safe boundaries. We should feel happy with the recent purchase. We should set goals and work toward them. We should give to causes graciously. We should, we should ... and yet we find it hard to do. Why is it that we know what we should do, or should feel, but many times end up feeling burdened, powerless, and guilty?

Many of our challenges are predictable responses, triggered by stress and anxiety, to experiences we have had with money in our past. We are not bad or broken—just human. Many of our financial beliefs and behaviors are based on what we have observed and experienced and how we have mentally and emotionally digested them.

We have all made financial mistakes. You may have sold your soul to the company store to bring in the hoped-for "mother lode." You may have gotten a stock tip at a party from a Wall Street guru that started out hot but quickly fizzled. You may have contributed to a charitable organization that you felt was going to use your money prudently, only to be severely disappointed. You may have made a big-ticket purchase you didn't need with money you didn't have to impress people you didn't like and felt the ache of regret.

People around you have undoubtedly failed and you felt the impact. Maybe it was a boss who lost the business and put you out of work, a salesperson who sold you the "sure thing" that wasn't, a family member whose decision negatively affected you, or a spouse who made a purchase you didn't discuss, causing consternation between you.

There is a lot of guilt and shame around finances, and it can keep you stuck in unhealthy patterns. In order to move forward with creating a healthy financial life, you need to understand and embrace who you are. Would it help to know that your brain is not wired to make wise financial choices consistently? Would it free you to know that humans have been making the same financial mistakes for centuries? Fear and greed, corticosterone and endorphins, and your past, present, and future selves continue to collide daily and play out in your decisions around work, investments, spending, and giving in ways that may not always be in your best interest.

What "money scripts" are you playing in your head? They may be positive and productive, or they may be negative and detrimental. The idea that your emotions, mental faculties, and financial behaviors are connected is a novel idea, one that can open the doors of transformation once grasped and accepted. For most of us, simple recognition, awareness, and training in how to dispel the lies in our heads, or how to build upon beneficial truths, will head us toward financial peace.

MONEY AND THE BRAIN

Our brains have a lot to do with how we deal with monetary issues and change. Dr. Brad Klontz and Dr. Ted Klontz have done in-depth research into how our reptilian, limbic, and emotional brains are organized and the effects on our thinking and behavior when it comes to money. Understanding and managing our rational and emotional minds is a very difficult thing to do. Not only do we need to look at ourselves, but we have families and layers upon layers of complexities to work through.

Remember the commercial with the catchphrase "This is your brain on drugs"? The field of neuroeconomics is rapidly shedding light on how our brains work "on money"—and how the reflexive and reflective components of our brains impact our decision making. It is fascinating to understand how the amygdala—one of the brain's centers for expressing fear—reacts when the market takes a precipitous plunge. Our reaction is similar to being chased by a lion, and we have the urge to flee—or sell, sell, sell!

The field of behavioral finance delves into how our brains affect our emotions and our behaviors around money. The biases that are inherent in our financial decision making include a loss-aversion bias. Studies have found that financial losses are felt between two and two-and-a-half times as strongly as financial gains.[24] Loss aversion favors inaction over action and the status quo over possible alterna-

---

24   Daniel Kahneman, Jack L. Knetsch, Richard H. Thaler, "Anomalies: The Endowment Effect, Loss Aversion, Status Quo Bias," *The Journal of Economic Perspectives* 5, no. 1: 193–206 (1991).

tives. Therefore, when it comes time for you to act on the gathered facts and analysis you have undertaken, unwarranted optimism and unreasonable risk aversion come into conflict. This bias can keep you stuck in a job you don't like, stay in a home you can't afford, or hold on to a losing investment longer than you should.

There will always be financial concerns. It's easy to look at the global, national, and local issues as they become fodder for talk shows and blogs and join in the lament. The hard part is to get personal and down to the nitty-gritty details of solving problems that concern you. We all have room to improve. It is easy to blame others, and ourselves, and resort to the path of least resistance—denial and status quo. But think of the improvements to be found by peeling off the candy coating of our financial lives and looking at the hidden causes of our pain, disenchantment, and restlessness. Are we willing to address financial flash points that have an emotional impact on us and are affecting our behavior? Are we bold enough to have safe conversations with spouses, family members, and trusted advisors about what we want to build on or what needs to change? We need new motivation to create financial health because if we have learned one thing from our societal and personal financial crises, it's that fear and shame don't work.

So what can we do? Well, the good news is that in today's world, we will never be without choice; but the bad news is that we may have too many choices. We can capitulate to our hardwired brains, or we can recognize the complexities, take a deep breath, and change the underpinnings of our decisions. We can create new neural pathways in our brains for how we think about and behave around money. We can also acknowledge that we make mistakes and then learn from them, let go of the guilt, and use our mental and emotional capacities along with technological advances to mitigate and manage what we do moving forward.

A small change in perspective can work wonders. The difference between saying "should do" and "choose to," is a powerful example. If you are living in a world of "should do," then you're keeping yourself in a position of pressure, capitulating to victimhood. What if you shift to the world of "choose to"? When you choose to do something, even if new or slightly new or uncomfortable, you are deciding to live in your own personal power and potential. Whatever financial decisions lie ahead for you, recognize that you are amazingly complex. Don't be afraid or ashamed to acknowledge that you have limitations, but don't accept that they are insurmountable, either. You can creatively, resourcefully, and strategically do your money differently. Do it one day at a time.

SHARPEN YOUR TOOLS

Look at what modifications you want to make in your life this year, whether they're physical, emotional, spiritual, or financial, and get to work putting together a "vision board" for what you want to see change about any, or all, of these areas in your life. Here are a few questions to get you started:

- 🍂 I am inspired to make changes because I know my children and their children will benefit. What's your inspiration? What is your one financial priority?

- 🍂 What does your ideal financial self and life look like?

- 🍂 What needs to change to get you 1 percent closer to your next best financial self? What action steps do you want to take on a daily basis?

CHAPTER 18

TIME TO TAKE ACTION

You don't have to be great to start, but you have to start to be great.

—ZIG ZIGLAR

After reading chapter after chapter, and learning about season after season, you are now far better equipped with the right tools, techniques, and mind-set to get the most from working from a competent financial life planner. He or she will continue to guide you through the more technical and personally customized elements of your financial journey. Even if you feel that you're qualified to blaze your own path, I recommend that you consult a professional at least periodically as your journey progresses. If you do want to seek out a financial advocate, guide, or advisor, what should you look for and consider?

Discuss and decide what you want to accomplish in an advisory relationship. Working with a financial planner helps you to stay on track in your financial life by adding a third-party perspective to your decision-making process. You will share your current situation and what is important now and down the road. Financial planners bring a deep understanding of technical components of products, financial markets, economic seasons, taxation issues, and more to bear for you. A good planner's goal is to help you banish fear, savor hope, and avoid regret with the financial component of life. Accomplishing clarity of vision and peace of mind in moving forward would be your goal.

As such, you have rights when working with a financial planner!

YOUR ADVISORY BILL OF RIGHTS

I.   You have the right to feel at ease with the planner you choose. You want to be able to communicate, to feel understood, and to understand.

II. You have the right to full disclosure by the advisor of any fees or commissions charged. If you are working with a Registered Investment Advisor, you should receive a copy of the advisor's ADV Part II—a document required by the SEC that outlines how their business is run and how they are compensated. It will include a code of ethics and privacy statement. You have a right to know what services you will be receiving and the cost of the services you are purchasing. What services are included in their asset management agreement? What is the scope of service in creating a financial plan, and what is the cost? How comprehensive is the planning process? Do they work with your other advisors? What is the time frame for completion of the plan as well as follow-up implementation? How often will your plan be reviewed?

III. You have the right to a written contract that spells out the terms of your working relationship. You or the planner should be able to discontinue the relationship if found to be inappropriate or unsatisfactory.

IV. You are entitled to written recommendations that are based on your individualized needs and goals. A customized plan will look at many aspects of your unique situation. The advisor works for you, and the better they know you, and every facet of your circumstances, the better they will serve you.

V. You have the right to confidentiality with regard to all information you provide to your planner. This is intimate territory and your personal life needs to be protected.

VI. You have the right to have your goals, objectives, and concerns treated with respect, with no value judgments made by the planner.

VII. You have the right to clear explanations for any and all recommendations and to thorough answers as to why those recommendations are being made. You should feel educated and empowered and confident that recommendations are in your best interest before you take action.

VIII. You have a right to assistance in the implementation of your plan, with your advisor working closely with everyone on your team. Without help in obtaining the appropriate tools to accomplish your intended strategies, your plan will remain another pile of papers on your desk.

IX. You have the right to an advisor who is available to you. You and your needs are important, and you have a right to be treated accordingly. You should have access to your advisor or their team to answer questions or get reassurance and support along the way.

In exchange for having your rights honored, you have the responsibility to work diligently and conscientiously with your advisor. You must be prepared to discuss your personal feelings, concerns, and objectives openly and honestly. You must bring all aspects of your financial life to the table to be incorporated into your plan. You must implement the agreed-upon actions in a timely fashion.

With the appropriate planner in place, you will be able to more wisely navigate the growing complexities of life transitions and the financial implications that arise from them.

As you traverse your personal financial seasons and engage in each economic season that unfolds, step forward bravely and boldly!

MY MONETARY MANIFESTO

1. **I will decide and hold tight to that which is important in my life.** I will work toward the understanding that money is a tool and, like the ecological seasons, is an integral part of experiencing life in its fullest expression. By recognizing its power and using it wisely, I will set in motion perennial growth for generations to come. Money is to be used constructively to build sustainable dynamics for my family and in my community. I will learn what

money means to me and how to use it properly in the context of expressing my values. My self-worth is not my net worth, and defining success beyond our bank account will unfold the beauty of each life season. I will free myself from the binds of the cultural and media insistence that "more is better" and that fulfillment comes solely from materialistic gain.

2. **I will consider how money comes into my life and the implications on creating true wealth.** It is no longer enough to just make a living, but I will work toward making a life. I will cultivate my passions, skills, and talents to the best of my ability and seek to earn an honest living that can provide for my needs and reasonable desires. As my life seasons change, I will maintain integrity in knowing what I have and how it is being used to facilitate a life well lived. I will live in gratitude and joy for the work opportunities I have, for the prospects to improve my condition and the abilities to gain knowledge and wisdom in all areas of my life.

3. **I will embrace giving as a foundational component of financial health.** I will wrestle with my demons of "not having enough" and move toward giving of my time, talent, and treasure creatively, graciously, and extravagantly. I will explore the causes that are important to me and create a plan that allows me to give systematically and intentionally. I will build some margin into my resources to give when an unexpected need arises in my family or community. By being intentional with my giving, I have permission to say no to other concerns without feeling guilty.

4. **I will spend less than I earn.** I will create a spending plan that reflects intention with my choices. I will not get to the end of the month and ask, "Where did it go?" I will set up times to talk with my spouse, partner, or friends so we can encourage and hold each other accountable. I will not take guilt trips but embark on a journey of constant course correction. I will fully enjoy the financial choices I choose within the safe spending boundaries that I create. I will discern between a soul need and an ego desire as I discern how to use the disposable income I have.

5. **I will reconnect with my financial vehicles.** I will know what I have, where it is, or track it down if necessary. I will know why I have the financial tools I own, what their purpose is, and what the costs associated with them are. I will understand how they work and make adjustments to them as new financial and personal seasons unfold.

6. **I will actively minimize my debt.** I cannot borrow my way to prosperity. I will establish a plan to pay off any consumer debt that is holding me hostage. I will not acquiesce to the belief that debt is normal and just the way it is. I am a victor, not a victim of my financial choices.

7. **I will care for and fully enjoy my possessions.** I will learn to appreciate and be content with what is in front of me. I will hold things lightly, letting go of that which is no longer serving me or bringing me joy.

8. **I will communicate with those in my life who are or may be affected by my financial decisions.** I will communicate openly and honestly about what I am trying to accomplish and why. I will provide the education to

help them understand the tools I am using and prepare them for future responsibilities. I will build a tribe that understands and believes that in employing money differently, intelligently, we can and will impact ourselves, our families, and the world.

Are you ready to revolutionize your financial life? We have explored ways to recognize your financial power, created with a mind-set of appreciation and abundance. We have shared ways to revitalize your financial power through understanding what you have, where it is, and how to use it wisely. We have opened ways to release your financial power through intentional giving, thoughtful investing, and prudent spending. It is up to you now. Step up and step into the growing assembly of like-minded people who want to view and use their money differently. You will heal wounds, build bridges, and create economies that endure and thrive. You will create and enjoy enduring personal and financial wealth for yourself, for your family, and for the benefit of others in your community and around the world.

Printed in the USA
CPSIA information can be obtained
at www.ICGtesting.com
JSHW012051140824
68134JS00035B/3375